When it comes to SEN and EHCPs, the system cor
when the Local Authority to agree your child ha
lengthy wait times to access the provision they a
needs.

In order to fully understanding your rights when it comes to SEN, you need an understanding of the relevant SEN law and guidance used by Local Authorities in England. It's worth spending a couple of hours learning the law to avoid stress at a later date in the process or when facing knockbacks.

Other useful sources of EHCP available online and via your local offer:

IPSEA.co.uk

SENDIASS - SEN advice services ran by each local Authority

SEN Solicitors - Can be useful for tribunal cases to get your child into the right school.

*Solicitors are an added expense and can prolong the process due to their route through the legal departments at the local authority.

SEND Tribunals - statistics

- 96% Success rate for families.
- £59.m public money wasted on lost SEND tribunals.
- 9,960 special school places could be funded each year with the money wasted on lost SEND tribunals.
- Nearly 3,500 disputed EHCP cases were withdrawn on conceded before they got to tribunal

As of January 2024, there are more than ½ million children and young people with EHCPs. With more than twice as many EHCPs issued in 2022 than in 2015. Research suggested this reflects both and awareness of SEN and parents and carers recognising that they need an EHCP in place for their child's needs to be adequately met.

What rules are local authorities supposed to be following when it comes to my child's SEN?

The local authorities follow rules set out by the government when it comes to their legal responsibilities

Some are **recommendations**, some are **statutory requirements** the local authorities' 'MUST' follow. You will notice the difference in wording in documents such as **'should'** vs **'must'**.

Where are the local authorities getting their guidance from specifically?

Together to Safeguard Children (2013): Statutory guidance from the Department for Education which sets Working out what is expected of organisations and individuals to safeguard and promote the welfare of children

The Childrens Act 1989 Guidance and Regulations Volume 2 (Care Planning Placement and Case Review) and Volume 3 (Planning Transition to Adulthood for Care Leavers): Guidance setting out the responsibilities of local authorities towards looked after children and care leavers .

Equality Act 2010: Advice for schools: Non-statutory advice from the Department for Education, produced to help schools understand how the Equality Act affects them and how to fulfil their duties under the Act

Reasonable adjustments for disabled pupils (2012): Technical guidance from the Equality and Human Rights Commission

Supporting pupils at school with medical conditions (2014): statutory guidance from the Department for Education •

The Mental Capacity Act Code of Practice: Protecting the vulnerable *you can access these online through google searches should you need to .*

The 3 main government legal documents underpinning SEN law are :

1. The special educational needs code of practice :SEND_Code_of_Practice_January_2015.pdf (publishing.service.gov.uk) Sometimes named the 'code of practice'. 292 pages

Special educational needs and disability code of practice: 0 to 25 years

Statutory guidance for organisations which work with and support children and young people who have special educational needs or disabilities

January 2015

2. The children and families act 2014 (part 3 mainly). Children and Families Act 2014 (legislation.gov.uk)

3. The equality Act 2010

We will be referring to the above throughout this book - The relevant parts underpinning SEN and EHCP rules are extracted for your reference.

The definition of Disability ……

Definition of disability under the Equality Act 2010

You're disabled under the Equality Act 2010 if you have a physical or mental impairment that has a 'substantial' and 'long-term' negative effect on your ability to do normal daily activities.

What does 'substantial' and 'long-term' mean'?

Substantial' is more than minor or trivial, eg it takes much longer than it usually would to complete a daily task like getting dressed 'long term' means 12 months or more, eg a breathing condition that develops as a result of a lung infection

Impairment and disability definition (The Act 2010)

A woman is obese. Her obesity in itself is not an impairment, but it causes breathing and mobility difficulties which substantially adversely affect her ability to walk.

A man has a borderline moderate learning disability which has an adverse impact on his short-term memory and his levels of literacy and numeracy. For example, he cannot write any original material, as opposed to slowly copying existing text, and he cannot write his address from memory.

It is the effects of these impairments that need to be considered, rather than the underlying conditions themselves.

More on disability ……………..

A young man has Attention Deficit Hyperactivity Disorder (ADHD) which manifests itself in a number of ways, including exhibitionism and an inability to concentrate. The disorder, as an impairment which has a substantial and long-term adverse effect on the young person's ability to carry out normal day-to-day activities, would be a disability for the purposes of the Act.
The young man is not entitled to the protection of the Act in relation to any discrimination he experiences as a consequence of his exhibitionism, because that is an excluded condition under the Act.

However, he would be protected in relation to any discrimination that he experiences in relation to the non-excluded effects of his condition, such as inability to concentrate. For example, he would be entitled to any reasonable adjustments that are required as a consequence of those effects. (the disability act 2010 A13)

How disabilities arise

A disability can arise from a wide range of impairments which can be:

sensory impairments, such as those affecting sight or hearing
impairments with fluctuating or recurring effects such as rheumatoid arthritis, myalgic encephalitis (ME), chronic fatigue syndrome (CFS), fibromyalgia, depression and epilepsy progressive, such as motor neurone disease, muscular dystrophy, and forms of dementia autoimmune conditions such as systemic lupus erythematosis (SLE) organ specific, including respiratory conditions, such as asthma, and cardiovascular diseases, including thrombosis, stroke and heart disease

- developmental, such as autistic spectrum disorders (ASD), dyslexia and dyspraxia
- learning disabilities
- mental health conditions with symptoms such as anxiety, low mood, panic attacks, phobias, or unshared perceptions; eating disorders; bipolar affective disorders; obsessive compulsive disorders; personality disorders; post traumatic stress disorder, and some selfharming behaviour
- mental illnesses, such as depression and schizophrenia
- produced by injury to the body, including to the brain

Now let's look at the definition of SEN Special educational needs (SEN)

A child or young person has SEN if they have a learning difficulty or disability which calls for special educational provision to be made for him or her.

Learning difficulty or disability definition

A child of compulsory school age or a young person has a learning difficulty or disability if he or she:

- has a significantly greater difficulty in learning than the majority of others of the same age, or

- has a disability which prevents or hinders him or her from making use of facilities of a kind generally provided for others of the same age in mainstream schools or mainstream post-16 institutions Now let's look at

- when a local authority must carry out an EHC needs assessment, including in response to a request

- who must be consulted and provide advice

- the statutory steps required by the process of EHC needs assessment and EHC plan development, including timescale

> **Relevant legislation**
>
> Primary
>
> Sections 36 – 50 of the Children and Families Act 2014
>
> The Care Act 2014
>
> Section 2 of the Chronically Sick and Disabled Persons Act 1970
>
> Sections 17, 20 and 47 of the Children Act 1989

The majority of children and young people with SEN or disabilities will have their needs met within local mainstream early years settings, schools or colleges.

Some children and young people may require an EHC needs assessment in order for the local authority to decide whether it is necessary for it to make provision in accordance with an EHC plan.

The purpose of an EHC plan is to make special educational provision to meet the special educational needs of the child or young person, to secure the best possible outcomes for them across education, health and social care and, as they get older, prepare them for adulthood.

If a child or young person has a learning difficulty or a disability which is holding them back at school or college, and the parents of the child or the young person (or the young person themselves) believe that the school or college is not able to provide the help and support which is needed, then a request should be made to the Local Authority ("LA") for an EHC needs assessment.

You can do this at any time.

You can only ask for an EHC needs assessment if the child or young person has, or may have, SEN – it does not apply where there are only health or social care needs. Remember that under the law, a child has SEN if they have a learning difficulty or a disability which calls for special educational provision.

Requesting an EHC needs assessment

Relevant legislation: Section 36 of the Children and Families Act 2014 9.8

The following people have a specific right to ask a local authority to conduct an education, health and care needs assessment for a child or young person aged between 0 and 25: 144

- the child's parent

- a young person over the age of 16 but under the age of 25, and

- a person acting on behalf of a school or post-16 institution (this should ideally be with the knowledge and agreement of the parent or young person where possible

(Usually the SENCO)

Other people who can apply

In addition, anyone else can bring a child or young person who has (or may have) SEN to the attention of the local authority, particularly where they think an EHC needs assessment may be necessary. This could include, for example, foster carers, health and social care professionals, early years practitioners, youth offending teams or probation services, those responsible for education in custody, school or college staff or a family friend. Bringing a child or young person to the attention of the local authority will be undertaken on an individual basis where there are specific concerns. This should be done with the knowledge and, where possible, agreement of the child's parent or the young person.

A local authority must conduct an assessment of education, health and care needs when it considers that it may be necessary for special educational provision to be made for the child or young person in accordance with an EHC plan.

In considering whether an EHC needs assessment is necessary, the local authority should consider whether there is evidence that despite the early years provider, school or post-16 institution having taken relevant and purposeful action to identify, assess and meet the special educational needs of the child or young person, the child or young person has not made expected progress.

To inform their decision the local authority will need to take into account a wide range of evidence, and should pay particular attention to:

- evidence of the child or young person's academic attainment (or developmental milestones in younger children) and rate of progress 146

- information about the nature, extent and context of the child or young person's SEN

- evidence of the action already being taken by the early years provider, school or post-16 institution to meet the child or young person's SEN

- evidence that where progress has been made, it has only been as the result of much additional intervention and support over and above that which is usually provided

Evidence of the child or young person's physical, emotional and social development and health needs, drawing on relevant evidence from clinicians and other health professionals and what has been done to meet these by other agencies, and

- where a young person is aged over 18, the local authority must consider whether the young person requires additional time, in comparison to the majority of others of the same age who do not have special educational needs, to complete their education or training. Remaining in formal education or training should help young people to achieve education and training outcomes, building on what they have learned before and preparing them for adult life

Local authorities must carry out their functions with a view to identifying all the children and young people in their area who have or may have SEN or have or may have a disability (Section 22 of the Children and Families Act 2014).

Local authorities may gather information on children and young people with SEN or disabilities in a number of ways. Anyone can bring a child or young person who they believe has or probably has SEN or a disability to the attention of a local authority (Section 24 of the Children and Families Act 2014) and parents, early years providers, schools and colleges have an important role in doing so.

CCGs, NHS Trusts and NHS Foundation Trusts must inform the appropriate local authority if they identify a child under compulsory school age as having, or probably having, SEN or a disability (Section 23 of the Children and Families Act 2014).

EHC plan creates legally binding obligations and upon whom.

Section 37 of the **children and families act** sets out what should be specified in an EHC plan;

Section 38 contains the duties on an LA in preparing a draft EHC plan; and

Section 42 of the Act contains the duties to secure the special educational provision and health care provision in accordance with an EHC plan.

What an EHCP contains -Section A

EHC plans must specify the special educational provision required to meet each of the child or young person's special educational needs

6. **What is an EHC plan – Section 37 of the Act**

Section 37

(2) For the purposes of this Part, an EHC plan is a plan specifying—

(a) the child's or young person's special educational needs;

(b) the outcomes sought for him or her;

(c) the special educational provision required by him or her;

(d) any health care provision reasonably required by the learning difficulties and disabilities which result in him or her having special educational needs;

(e) in the case of a child or a young person aged under 18, any social care provision which must be made for him or her by the local authority as a result of section 2 of the Chronically Sick and Disabled Persons Act 1970

(as it applies in section 28A of that Act);

(f) any social care provision reasonably required by the learning difficulties and disabilities which result in the child or young person having special educational needs, to the extent that the provision is not already specified in the plan under paragraph (e).

(3) An EHC plan may also specify other health care and social care provision reasonably required by the child or young person.

The first words of this section, therefore, qualify everything which follows: an EHC plan is a plan which "specifies" all of the sections described. Case law has established that a duty to specify means that wording must be so specific and so clear as to leave no room for doubt as to what has been decided in necessary in the individual case.

This duty therefore applies to all of the sections of the EHC plan set out in Section 37(2) of the Act.

Needs

The EHC plan is required by (section 37(2)(a) of the Act) to specify the child's special educational needs. However, section 37 does not require the health needs or the social care needs to be specified in the EHC plan, only the special educational needs.

An EHC plan must specify the "outcomes sought" for the child or young person (section 37(2)(b) of the Act). These are a key part of an EHC plan and should derive from the advice obtained during the EHC needs assessment.

"Reasonably required". This is an important point to grasp. Where special educational provision is concerned, if it is required then it must be specified in the plan.

However, this is not the case with health care provision.

In relation to Health Care Provision there is another important caveat to be aware of which is contained in SEN Reg 12(2). The health care provision must be agreed by the responsible commissioning body before it can be included in an EHC plan.

"Special educational provision", for a child aged two or more or a young person, means educational or training provision that is additional to, or different from, that made generally for others of the same age in—

(a) mainstream schools in England,

(b) maintained nursery schools in England,

(c) mainstream post-16 institutions in England, or

(d) places in England at which relevant early years education is provided.

Health care provision is defined as follows:

Section 21(3) "Health care provision" means the provision of health care services as part of the comprehensive health service in England   Social care provision is defined as follows:

Section 21(4) ."Social care provision" means the provision made by a local authority in the exercise of its social services functions.

These different types of provision are differentiated by the source of the provision. But in relation to health care provision and social care provision this is subject to section 21(5):

Section 21(5)

Health care provision or social care provision which educates or trains a child or young person is to be treated as special educational provision (instead of health care provision or social care provision). – this is important for OT for example, say a child needs Occupational therapy the funding comes from either heath or education depending on if it, 'educates' or
'trains'.

This is considered in more detail below under the comments about Section F of an EHC plan.

The EHC plan may also specify other health care or social care provision reasonably required by the child or young person.

Having reviewed the framework of an EHC plan from the Act, consideration of how to analyse an EHC plan in detail is set out below.

There is no standard form of an EHC plan but SEN Reg 12 contains detailed requirements of what the LA must set out in an EHC plan in separate sections and referred to by designated letters. This is reflected in the Code.

Section	Information to include
(A) The views, interests and aspirations of the child and their parents, or of the young person	- Details about the child or young person's aspirations and goals for the future (but not details of outcomes to be achieved – see section above on outcomes for guidance). When agreeing the aspirations, consideration should be given to the child or young person's aspirations for paid employment, independent living and community participation - Details about play, health, schooling, independence, friendships, further education and future plans including employment (where practical) - A summary of how to communicate with the child or young person and engage them in decision-making. - The child or young person's history - If written in the first person, the plan should make clear whether the child or young person is being quoted directly, or if the views of parents or professionals are being represented

Sections B and C.

Section	Information to include
(B) The child or young person's special educational needs (SEN)	- All of the child or young person's identified special educational needs **must** be specified - SEN may include needs for health and social care provision that are treated as special educational provision

Section	Information to include
(C) The child or young person's health needs which relate to their SEN	- The EHC plan **must** specify any health needs identified through the EHC needs assessment which relate to the child or young person's SEN. Some health care needs, such as routine dental health needs, are unlikely to be related - The Clinical Commissioning Group (CCG) may also choose to specify other health care needs which are not related to the child or young person's SEN (for example, a long-term condition which might need management in a special educational setting)

Section D

(D) The child or young person's social care needs which relate to their SEN	- The EHC plan **must** specify any social care needs identified through the EHC needs assessment which relate to the child or young person's SEN or which require provision for a child or young person under 18 under section 2 of the Chronically Sick and Disabled Persons Act 1970
- The local authority may also choose to specify other social care needs which are not linked to the child or young person's SEN or to a disability. This could include reference to any child in need or child protection plan which a child may have relating to other family issues such as neglect. Such an approach could help the child and their parents manage the different plans and bring greater co-ordination of services. Inclusion **must** only be with the consent of the child and their parents

Section E

(E) The outcomes sought for the child or the young person	- A range of outcomes over varying timescales, covering education, health and care as appropriate but recognising that it is the education and training outcomes only that will help determine when a plan is ceased for young people aged over 18. Therefore, for young people aged over 17, the EHC plan should identify clearly which outcomes are education and training outcomes. See paragraph 9.64 onwards for more detail on outcomes
- A clear distinction between outcomes and provision. The provision should help the child or young person achieve an outcome, it is not an outcome in itself
- Steps towards meeting the outcomes
- The arrangements for monitoring progress, including review and transition review arrangements and the arrangements for setting and monitoring shorter term

Section F

Most people don't realise this really is the most important bit of the EHCP – what will your child 'get' to meet their needs. Wording has to be careful here. Don't panic if there is not a specified 1:1 adult here, it's what most parents wany but in reality, that's not what you see. What that looks like is your child will likely need 1:1 important parts of the day. There might be a few children in the class with a variety of needs. They may be led by a teaching assistant who will be directed by the teacher.

If you child is in a special school, they will be in a small group led by a special needs teacher who is directed and informed by therapists and other professionals so 1:1 is not always helpful – better planning is better than an untrained, 'Velcro' adult.

If you child is a, 'runner' or has no sense of danger or has mobility barriers they may need a full-time adult for safety but again they don't and shouldn't be joined at the hip creating dependency issues and hindering independence.

- The plan should specify:
    - any appropriate facilities and equipment, staffing arrangements and curriculum
    - any appropriate modifications to the application of the National Curriculum, where relevant
    - any appropriate exclusions from the application of the National Curriculum or the course being studied in a post-16 setting, in detail, and the provision which it is proposed to substitute for any such exclusions in order to maintain a balanced and broadly based curriculum
    - where residential accommodation is appropriate,

Section	Information to include
	that fact
	○ where there is a Personal Budget, the outcomes to which it is intended to contribute (detail of the arrangements for a Personal Budget, including any direct payment, **must** be included in the plan and these should be set out in section J)
	• See paragraph 9.131 onwards for details of duties on the local authority to maintain the special educational provision in the EHC plan

Section G

(G) Any health provision reasonably required by the learning difficulties or disabilities which result in the child or young person having SEN	<ul><li>Provision should be detailed and specific and should normally be quantified, for example, in terms of the type of support and who will provide it</li><li>It should be clear how the provision will support achievement of the outcomes, including the health needs to be met and the outcomes to be achieved through provision secured through a personal (health) budget</li><li>Clarity as to how advice and information gathered has informed the provision specified</li><li>Health care provision reasonably required may include specialist support and therapies, such as medical treatments and delivery of medications, occupational therapy and physiotherapy, a range of nursing support, specialist equipment, wheelchairs and continence supplies. It could include highly specialist services needed by only a small number of children which are commissioned centrally by NHS England (for example therapeutic provision for young offenders in the secure estate)</li><li>The local authority and CCG may also choose to specify other health care provision reasonably required by the child or young person, which is not linked to their learning difficulties or disabilities, but which should sensibly be co-ordinated with other services in the plan</li><li>See paragraph 9.141 for details of duties on the health service to maintain the health care provision in the EHC plan</li></ul>

Section H

(H1) Any social care provision which must be made for a child or young person under 18 resulting from	<ul><li>Provision should be detailed and specific and should normally be quantified, for example, in terms of the type of support and who will provide it (including where this is to be secured through a social care direct payment)</li><li>It should be clear how the provision will support achievement of the outcomes, including any provision</li></ul>

Section H continued

	Chronically Sick and Disabled Persons Act 1970 (CSDPA)	clarity as to how advice and information gathered has informed the provision specified
		• Section H1 of the EHC plan **must** specify all services assessed as being needed for a disabled child or young person under 18, under section 2 of the CSDPA. These services include:
		    ○ practical assistance in the home
		    ○ provision or assistance in obtaining recreational and educational facilities at home and outside the home
		    ○ assistance in travelling to facilities
		    ○ adaptations to the home
		    ○ facilitating the taking of holidays
		    ○ provision of meals at home or elsewhere
		    ○ provision or assistance in obtaining a telephone and any special equipment necessary
		    ○ non-residential short breaks (included in Section H1 on the basis that the child as well as his or her parent will benefit from the short break)
		• This may include services to be provided for parent carers of disabled children, including following an assessment of their needs under sections 17ZD-17ZF of the Children Act 1989
		• See paragraph 9.137 onwards for details of duties on local authorities to maintain the social care provision in the EHC plan

Section I

	(I) Placement	• The name *and* type of the school, maintained nursery school, post-16 institution or other institution to be attended by the child or young person and the type of that institution (or, where the name of a school or other institution is not specified in the EHC plan, the type of school or other institution to be attended by the child or young person) • These details **must** be included only in the final EHC plan, *not* the draft EHC plan sent to the child's parent or to the young person • See paragraph 9.78 onwards for more details

Section J

(J) Personal Budget (including arrangements for direct payments)	•	This section should provide detailed information on any Personal Budget that will be used to secure provision in the EHC plan
	•	It should set out the arrangements in relation to direct payments as required by education, health and social care regulations
	•	The special educational needs and outcomes that are to be met by any direct payment **must** be specified
(K) Advice and information	•	The advice and information gathered during the EHC needs assessment **must** be set out in appendices to the EHC plan. There should be a list of this advice and information

What if child is refused and EHCP?

The LA must reply within six weeks (this is required by regulation 4(1) of the Special Educational Needs and Disability Regulations 2014). They should always reply to you as a parent or young person – even where the request was made by the school or college.

You can ask for information from the school and LA which may help you evidence that the test for an EHC needs assessment is met. If you did not have this information when you made your request, you could submit any helpful evidence you obtain before the LA's decision is due and ask the LA to consider it.

Make a note of the six week deadline for the LA's reply. If they do not respond in time, you email a complaint.

If the LA refuses to carry out an assessment, you have the right to appeal against this decision. The letter should explain that there is a right to appeal to the First-tier Tribunal (Special Educational Needs and Disability), and should contain details of a mediation service for you to contact.

What is the time limit for the local authority to respond to a request for assessment?

A local authority ("**LA**") is required to notify you of its decision on your request for assessment within 6 weeks of receiving it.

When does the time limit start?

The 6 week time limit runs from the date on which the LA **receives** the request for assessment. When it is classed as 'received' will depend on the method used to send it. If it is:

1. Delivered by hand, the 6 weeks runs from the day of delivery (or the following working day if it is delivered after 5pm or on a nonworking day);
2. Sent by signed for delivery, the 6 weeks runs from the date on which a representative of the LA signs for it (you will be able to check online when the item was delivered);
3. Sent by first class post, the 6 weeks runs from the next working day after it was posted;
4. Sent by e-mail, the 6 weeks runs from the day that it is sent (or the following working day if it is sent after 5pm or on a

nonworking day).

Are there exceptions to the time limit?

There are some circumstances in which an LA may not be required to comply with the 6 week time limit if it would be impractical for it to do so. These are where:

(a)   The LA asks for advice about the request from a school, college or early years provider during a time when it is closed for a period of longer than 4 weeks (i.e. in the summer holidays), or in the week before it closes for such a period.

(b)   During the six week period, exceptional personal circumstances affect the child, the child's parent or the young person or they are away for more than 4 weeks.

The LA will only be able to rely on one of these exceptions if it can show that making the decision on time would be impractical. The LA is still required to notify you of its decision on your request as soon as possible.

When should I complain?

You should complain as soon as the 6 week period has expired.

The Mental Capacity Act 8.19

The Mental Capacity Act 8.19 The right of young people to make a decision is subject to their capacity to do so as set out in the Mental Capacity Act 2005. The underlying principle of the Act is to ensure that those who lack capacity are empowered to make as many decisions for themselves as possible and that any decision made or action taken on their behalf is done so in their best interests.

Decisions about mental capacity are made on an individual basis, and may vary according to the nature of the decision. Someone who may lack capacity to make a decision in one area of their life may be able to do so in another. There is further guidance on the Mental Capacity Act and how it applies both to parents and to young people in relation to the Act in Annex 1, Mental Capacity

The role of the SENCO involves: ensuring all practitioners in the setting understand their responsibilities to children with SEN and the setting's approach to identifying and meeting SEN

- advising and supporting colleagues

- ensuring parents are closely involved throughout and that their insights inform action taken by the setting, and

- liaising with professionals or agencies beyond the setting School

Admissions

With a national shortage of special school places, lack of resources to properly staff them and closure of lots of residential schools I would keep options open when it comes to school choice. Since the government started to build, 'units' or 'provisions' attached to mainstream schools, the landscape has changed. Originally designed to cater for those with moderate needs who access mainstream education with support, they are often more like mini special schools due to the level of need and the addition of specialist teachers. You must look around a school first, I know so many parents who think they want the outstanding special school for their child only to visit and change their minds once they have been to visit.

Mainstreams for SEMH needs with authority blanket behaviour policies don't often work for children needing flexibly but they can adapt with the right home guidance.

A right to mainstream education

Section 33 CAFA 2014 says that a child or young person with an EHC plan be educated in a mainstream setting unless: it is against the wishes of the child's parent or the young person; or it is **incompatible with the provision of efficient education for others that there are no reasonable steps that it could take to prevent the incompatibility.**

The fundamental principle underpinning the law is that where a parent of a child with SEN, or a young person with SEN, wants a place in a mainstream setting it must never be denied it on the basis that mainstream is unsuitable, or that their needs or disabilities are too great or complex. Inclusive education is one of the principles stated to underpin the SEN and Disability Code of Practice (the "**Code**").

Whatever the law says, some parents meet mainstream schools that are unwelcoming and attempt to dissuade them from applying for admission. The Code says (paragraph 1.27):

"The School Admissions Code of Practice requires children and young people with SEN to be treated fairly. Admissions authorities:

- **must** consider applications from parents of children who have SEN but do not have an EHC plan on the basis of the school's published admissions criteria as part of normal admissions procedures
- **must not** refuse to admit a child who has SEN but does not have an EHC plan because they do not feel able to cater for those needs
- **must not** refuse to admit a child on the grounds that they do not have an EHC plan."

There can be a long wait for your child to be transferred to a different school. Taking them out school make seem easier however after a few weeks this may not be sustainable for you and them.

Disputes with schools.

Over the years I have seen so many parents 'waiting' for a special school. This wait can be up to 2 years, from initial agreement to actually finding a place. It's important that the school and parent don't just stop trying anything until a space comes up. Those 2 years must not be all about waitin; but trying interventions.

There are different options :

1. Keep them in school and work with the school to support your child.

2. EHE- Elective Home educating – you won't get much support or access to provision so make sure you think this through. The school and LA are effectively no longer responsible for providing provision, **you are** as they are no longer responsible. You still have Annual reviews but the provision is up to you to fund.

If you have a disagreement with a school and you feel you are not being fairly treated, I would always recommend meeting with the SENCO and Head and trying to come to a compromise. It's in both your interests to make it work.

Schools cannot exclude children without having tried lots of interventions first. It's better you work with them to come up with ideas, being the expert in knowing your child that face further conflict and added stress to what is likely to be a very stressful time.

Try using these sorts of phrases where you only discuss their needs and how to support them it prevents the 'blame' argument coming up! For example, if your child is not coping in class due to large groups and is disruptive/refusing to work/arguing/fighting (fight or flight) .

"She can't cope in large groups especial when demands are put upon her, this triggers her into challenging behaviour. She's better starting the lesson with a small easy task she can access then move onto a small piece of work, with a break card to request for a break if she needs one"   you are suggesting provision /intervention to be in place to support her needs.

By suggesting this, if you get the phone call the next day you can go back to the 'behaviour support plan' above, did the teacher put too many demands of her? was the task too hard? what she allowed a break? these simple things might work rather than a whole change of school. This outcome is better for the child and the school who want to be able to support your child although it might not seem it at first.

Try and do this but if it's too much and they continue to blame your child for their behaviour an EHCP will help. Sadly, many schools don't know how to support lots of children, you need to work with them and try to stay calm. You are the expert and schools are not focused on learning better ways to work **with** families.

You may not want to change your parenting style but it's important you too listen to what the professionals or educational psychologists recommend. Are you putting boundaries in place? Even the most serve non-verbal autism children can be supported in managing their behaviours, you too must be willing to be told how to parent just as the school will need to follow their guidance. This can be the most difficult part of SEN parenting. Especially SEMH children who may need a completely ridged consistent secure parenting style. If this does not come naturally to you, if they are refusing to do anything you say, you can also try to implement things at home to make yours and their lives easier. If your child has attachment difficulties, the educational psychologist can be accessed for the SENCO for advice/assessment/Training.

It's good teaching for the child too. Think of it this way, if your child enters a shop, throws the toys off the shelf, screams and tries to open the sweets. what should you do?

a) Never take them to a shop again

b) Keep going back until they learn

c) Talk about shop rules, show them pictures and prepare them for the trip, take a shopping list they can tick off items with as they go around, reward them at the end for waiting etc

i.e -teach them how to do it properly.

its C- think of this with schools – it might feel like there's nothing you can do but try as many things as you can and don't expect results overnight. If you can get the school on board trying things then you won't have to. They are all teachers some have training in SEN some don't but you can work with them as a team. It's called the, 'graduated approach' and is well-known good practice.

Having an EHCP doesn't stop things going wrong, you need to work with schools throughout. Sometimes and EHCP and a new school is not the only answer. See what resources you already have – a school place? A teacher ? SENCO ? these are all your resources you can work **with** to support your child.

The legal bit-

School admission

The School Admissions Code of Practice requires children and young people with SEN to be treated fairly. Admissions authorities:

- must consider applications from parents of children who have SEN but do not have an EHC plan on the basis of the school's published admissions criteria as part of normal admissions procedures

- must not refuse to admit a child who has SEN but does not have an EHC plan because they do not feel able to cater for those needs

- must not refuse to admit a child on the grounds that they do not have an EHC plan

Children without an EHCP going to special schools

Children and young people without an EHC plan can be placed in special schools and special post-16 institutions only in the following exceptional circumstances:

- where they are admitted to a special school or special post-16 institution to be assessed for an EHC plan with their agreement (in the case of a young person) or the agreement of their parent (in the case of a child), the local authority, the head teacher or principal of the special school or special post-16 institution and anyone providing advice for the assessment

- where they are admitted to a special school or special post-16 institution following a change in their circumstances with their agreement (in the case of a young person) or the agreement of their parent (in the case of a child), the local authority and the head teacher or principal of the special school or special post-16 institution. Where an emergency placement of this kind is made the local authority should immediately initiate an EHC needs assessment or re-assessment

- where they are in hospital and admitted to a special school which is established in a hospital, or • where they are admitted to a special academy (including a special free school) whose academy arrangements allow it to admit children or young people with SEN who do not have an EHC plan 27

Where else to seek help for free:

> When you don't have an EHCP-Try to resolve disputes with schools via the SENCO. This is a less invasive, less stressful way of mediating the issue and will be less disruptive. Also utilise www.ipsea.co.uk

When you have an

EHCP

Try to speak to the SENCO, then Case Officer

> You can call sendiass, an impartial free advice service, every local authority has one.

1. SEN Lawyers – can be an added expense however decide on what is best for your case.

2. the rest of this book's details specifically the EHCP and the law relating to it.

Annotations explained.

In order to make the Act more accessible, annotations have been made to explain the most important parts of the Act when communicative with local authorities. There are various sections of the act you will find are often referred to when provision is disputed.

In red – important statements to refer to and think about when disputes occur around the type of provision your child is entitled to. In Blue - explanations.

THE CHILDREN AND FAMILIES ACT 2014

7. **PART 3**

CHILDREN AND YOUNG PEOPLE IN ENGLAND WITH SPECIAL EDUCATIONAL NEEDS OR DISABILITIES

Local authority functions: general principles

19 Local authority functions: supporting and involving children and young people

In exercising a function under this Part in the case of a child or young person, a local authority in England must have regard to the following matters in particular—

(a) the views, wishes and feelings of the child and his or her parent, or the young person;

(b) the importance of the child and his or her parent, or the young person, participating as fully as possible in decisions relating to the exercise of the function concerned;

(c) the importance of the child and his or her parent, or the young person, being provided with the information and support necessary to enable participation in those decisions;

(d) the need to support the child and his or her parent, or the young person, in order to facilitate the development of the child or young person and to help him or her achieve the best possible educational and other outcomes.

Special educational needs etc

20 When a child or young person has special educational needs A child or young person has special educational needs if he or she has a learning difficulty or disability which calls for special educational provision (educational or training provision that is additional to, or different from, that made generally for others of the same age in mainstream schools in England,)

(1)   to be made for him or her.

If you are refused an EHCP, its often that the school can provide what they need but if you can prove they need educational (not a health provision) that is more than those in their class i.e speech therapy that can't ordinarily be provided they will qualify for a needs assessment (the bit before the EHCP is issued)

A learning difficult is defined as

(2)   A child of compulsory school age or a young person has a learning difficulty or disability if he or she—

(a)**has a significantly greater difficulty in learning** than the majority of others of the same age, or

(b)has a disability which prevents or hinders him or her from making use of facilities of a **kind generally provided for others of the same age in mainstream schools or mainstream post-16 institutions.**

(3)   A child under compulsory school age has a learning difficulty or disability if he or she is likely to be within subsection (2) when of compulsory school age (or would be likely, if no special educational provision were made).

(4)   A child or young person does not have a learning difficulty or disability solely because the language (or form of language) in which he or she is or will be taught is different from a language (or form of language) which is or has been spoken at home.

(5)This section applies for the purposes of this Part.

21 Special educational provision, health care provision and social care provision

(1)"Special educational provision", for a child aged two or more or a young person, means educational or training provision that is additional to, or different from, that made generally for others of the same age in—
(a)mainstream schools in England,

(b) maintained nursery schools in England,

(c) mainstream post-16 institutions in England, or

(d) places in England at which relevant early years education is provided.

(2) "Special educational provision", for a child aged under two, means educational provision of any kind.

(3) "Health care provision" means the provision of health care services as part of the comprehensive health service in England continued under section 1(1) of the National Health Service Act 2006.

(4) "Social care provision" means the provision made by a local authority in the exercise of its social services functions.

(5) Health care provision or social care provision which educates or trains a child or young person is to be treated as special educational provision (instead of health care provision or social care provision).

(6) This section applies for the purposes of this Part.

Identifying children and young people with special educational needs and disabilities

22 Identifying children and young people with special educational needs and disabilities

A local authority in England must exercise its functions with a view to securing that it identifies—

(a) all the children and young people in its area who have or **may have** special educational needs, and

(b) all the children and young people in its area who have a disability.

23 Duty of health bodies to bring certain children to local authority's attention

(1) This section applies where, in the course of exercising functions in relation to a child who is under compulsory school age, a clinical commissioning group, NHS trust or NHS foundation trust form the opinion that the child has (or probably has) special educational needs or a disability.

(2) The group or trust must—

(a) inform the child's parent of their opinion and of their duty under subsection (3), and

(b) give the child's parent an opportunity to discuss their opinion with an officer of the group or trust.

(3) The group or trust must then bring their opinion to the attention of the appropriate local authority in England.

(4) If the group or trust think a particular voluntary organisation is likely to be able to give the parent advice or assistance in connection with any special educational needs or disability the child may have, they must inform the parent of that.

Children and young people for whom a local authority is responsible

24 When a local authority is responsible for a child or young person
(1) A local authority in England is responsible for a child or young person if he or she is in the authority's area and has been—

(a) identified by the authority as someone who has or **may have** special educational needs, or

(b) brought to the authority's attention by any person as someone who has or may have special educational needs.

(2) This section applies for the purposes of this Part.

Education, health and care provision: integration and joint commissioning

The next section really applies to local authorities only and is rarely relevant to school and parents/carers directly :

25 Promoting integration
(1) A local authority in England must exercise its functions under this Part with a view to ensuring the integration of educational provision and training provision with health care provision and social care provision, where it thinks that this would—

(a) promote the well-being of children or young people in its area who have special educational needs or a disability, or

(b) improve the quality of special educational provision—

(i) made in its area for children or young people who have special educational needs, or

(ii) made outside its area for children or young people for whom it is responsible who have special educational needs.

(2) The reference in subsection (1) to the well-being of children and young people is to their well-being so far as relating to—

(a) physical and mental health and emotional well-being;

(b) protection from abuse and neglect;

(c) control by them over their day-to-day lives;

(d) participation in education, training or recreation;

(e) social and economic well-being;

(f) domestic, family and personal relationships; (g) the contribution made by them to society.

26 Joint commissioning arrangements

(1) A local authority in England and its partner commissioning bodies must make arrangements ("joint commissioning arrangements") about the education, health and care provision to be secured for—

(a) children and young people for whom the authority is responsible who have special educational needs, and

(b) children and young people in the authority's area who have a disability.

(2) In this Part "education, health and care provision" means—

(a) special educational provision;

(b) health care provision; (c) social care provision.

(3) Joint commissioning arrangements must include arrangements for considering and agreeing—

(a) the education, health and care provision reasonably required by—

(i) the learning difficulties and disabilities which result in the children and young people within subsection (1)(a) having special educational needs, and

(ii) the disabilities of the children and young people within subsection (1)(b);

(b) what education, health and care provision is to be secured;

(c) by whom education, health and care provision is to be secured;

(d) what advice and information is to be provided about education, health and care provision;

(e)by whom, to whom and how such advice and information is to be provided;

(f)how complaints about education, health and care provision may be made and are to be dealt with;

(g)procedures for ensuring that disputes between the parties to the joint commissioning arrangements are resolved as quickly as possible.

(4)Joint commissioning arrangements about securing education, health and care provision must in particular include arrangements for—

(a)securing EHC needs assessments;

(b)securing the education, health and care provision specified in EHC plans;

(c)agreeing personal budgets under section 49.

(5)Joint commissioning arrangements may also include other provision.

(6)The parties to joint commissioning arrangements must—

(a)have regard to them in the exercise of their functions, and

(b)keep them under review.

(7)Section 116B of the Local Government and Public Involvement in Health Act 2007 (duty to have regard to assessment of relevant needs and joint health and wellbeing strategy) applies in relation to functions exercisable under this section.

(8)A local authority's "partner commissioning bodies" are—

(a)the National Health Service Commissioning Board, to the extent that it is under a duty under section 3B of the National Health Service Act 2006 to arrange for the provision of services or facilities for—

(i)any children and young people for whom the authority is responsible who have special educational needs, or

(ii)any children and young people in the authority's area who have a disability, and

(b)each clinical commissioning group that is under a duty under section 3 of that Act to arrange for the provision of services or facilities for any children and young people within paragraph (a).

(9)Regulations may prescribe circumstances in which a clinical commissioning group that would otherwise be a partner commissioning body of a local authority by virtue of subsection (8)(b) is to be treated as not being a partner commissioning body of the authority.

Review of education and care provision

27 Duty to keep education and care provision under review

(1) A local authority in England must keep under review—

(a) the educational provision, training provision and social care provision made in its area for children and young people who have special educational needs or a disability, and

(b) the educational provision, training provision and social care provision made outside its area for—

(i) children and young people for whom it is responsible who have special educational needs, and

(ii) children and young people in its area who have a disability.

(2) The authority must consider the extent to which the provision referred to in subsection (1)(a) and (b) is sufficient to meet the educational needs, training needs and social care needs of the children and young people concerned.

(3) In exercising its functions under this section, the authority must consult—

(a) children and young people in its area with special educational needs, and the parents of children in its area with special educational needs;

(b) children and young people in its area who have a disability, and the parents of children in its area who have a disability;

(c) the governing bodies of maintained schools and maintained nursery schools in its area;

(d) the proprietors of Academies in its area;

(e) the governing bodies, proprietors or principals of post-16 institutions in its area;

(f) the governing bodies of non-maintained special schools in its area;

(g) the advisory boards of children's centres in its area;

(h) the providers of relevant early years education in its area;

(i)the governing bodies, proprietors or principals of other schools and post-16 institutions in England and Wales that the authority thinks are or are likely to be attended by—

(i)children or young people for whom it is responsible, or

(ii)children or young people in its area who have a disability;

(j)a youth offending team that the authority thinks has functions in relation to—

(i)children or young people for whom it is responsible, or

(ii)children or young people in its area who have a disability; (k)such

other persons as the authority thinks appropriate.

(4)Section 116B of the Local Government and Public Involvement in Health Act 2007 (duty to have regard to **assessment of relevant needs** and joint health and wellbeing strategy) applies in relation to functions exercisable under this section.

(5)"Children's centre" has the meaning given by section 5A(4) of the Childcare Act 2006.

Co-operation and assistance

28Co-operating generally: local authority functions

(1)A local authority in England must **co-operate with each of its local partners**, and each local partner must co-operate with the authority, in the exercise of the authority's functions under this Part.

This means that schools must reply to local authority emails and requests in a timely manor – as do the professionals such as education phycologists and speech therapists so they are all working together and nothing is missed .Due to improvements in technology this is rarely an issue in 2024.

(2)Each of the following is a local partner of a local authority in England for this purpose—

(a)where the authority is a county council for an area for which there is also a district council, the district council;

(b)the governing body of a maintained school or maintained nursery school that is maintained by the authority or provides education or training for children or young people for whom the authority is responsible;

(c)the proprietor of an Academy that is in the authority's area or provides education or training for children or young people for whom the authority is responsible;

(d)the proprietor of a non-maintained special school that is in the authority's area or provides education or training for children or young people for whom the authority is responsible;

(e)the governing body of an institution within the further education sector that is in the authority's area, or is attended, or likely to be attended, by children or young people for whom the authority is responsible;

(f)the management committee of a pupil referral unit that is in the authority's area, or is in England and is or is likely to be attended by children or young people for whom the authority is responsible;

(g)the proprietor of an institution approved by the Secretary of State under section 41 (independent special schools and special post 16 institutions: approval) that is in the authority's area, or is attended, or likely to be attended, by children or young people for whom the authority is responsible;

(h)any other person (other than a school or post-16 institution) that makes special educational provision for a child or young person for whom the authority is responsible;

(i)a youth offending team that the authority thinks has functions in relation to children or young people for whom it is responsible;

(j)a person in charge of relevant youth accommodation—

(i)in which there are detained persons aged 18 or under for whom the authority was responsible immediately before the beginning of their detention, or

(ii)that the authority thinks is accommodation in which such persons are likely to be detained;

(k)the National Health Service Commissioning Board;

(l)a clinical commissioning group—

(i)whose area coincides with, or falls wholly or partly within, the authority's area, or

(ii)which is under a duty under section 3 of the National Health Service Act 2006 to arrange for the provision of services or facilities for any children and young people for whom the authority is responsible;

(m) an NHS trust or NHS foundation trust which provides services in the authority's area, or which exercises functions in relation to children or young people for whom the authority is responsible;

(n) a Local Health Board which exercises functions in relation to children or young people for whom the authority is responsible.

(3) A local authority in England must make arrangements for ensuring cooperation between—

(a) the officers of the authority who exercise the authority's functions relating to education or training,

(b) the officers of the authority who exercise the authority's social services functions for children or young people with special educational needs, and

(c) the officers of the authority, so far as they are not officers within paragraph (a) or (b), who exercise the authority's functions relating to provision which is within section 30(2)(e) (provision to assist in preparing children and young people for adulthood and independent living).

(4) Regulations may prescribe circumstances in which a clinical commissioning group that would otherwise be a local partner of a local authority by virtue of subsection (2)(l)(ii) is to be treated as not being a local partner of the authority.

29 Co-operating generally: governing body functions

(1) This section applies where an appropriate authority for a school or post-16 institution mentioned in subsection (2) has functions under this Part.

(2) The schools and post-16 institutions referred to in subsection (1) are—

(a) mainstream schools;

(b) maintained nursery schools;

(c) 16 to 19 Academies;

(d) institutions within the further education sector;

(e) pupil referral units;

(f) alternative provision Academies.

(3) The appropriate authority must co-operate with each responsible local authority, and each responsible local authority must co-operate with the appropriate authority, in the exercise of those functions.

(4) A responsible local authority, in relation to an appropriate authority for a school or post-16 institution mentioned in subsection (2), is a local authority in England that is responsible for any child or young person who is a registered pupil or a student at the school or post-16 institution.

(5) The "appropriate authority" for a school or post-16 institution is—

(a) in the case of a maintained school, maintained nursery school, or institution within the further education sector, the governing body;

(b) in the case of an Academy, the proprietor;

(c) in the case of a pupil referral unit, the management committee.

Information and advice

30 Local offer

(1) A local authority in England must publish information about—

(a) the provision within subsection (2) it expects to be available in its area at the time of publication for children and young people who have special educational needs or a disability, and

(b) the provision within subsection (2) it expects to be available outside its area at that time for—

(i) children and young people for whom it is responsible, and

(ii) children and young people in its area who have a disability.

(2) The provision for children and young people referred to in subsection (1) is—

(a) education, health and care provision;

(b) other educational provision;

(c) other training provision;

(d) arrangements for travel to and from schools and post-16 institutions and places at which relevant early years education is provided;

(e) provision to assist in preparing children and young people for adulthood and independent living.

(3) For the purposes of subsection (2)(e), provision to assist in preparation for adulthood and independent living includes provision relating to—

(a) finding employment; (b) obtaining accommodation; (c) participation in society.

(4) Information required to be published by an authority under this section is to be known as its "local offer".

(5) A local authority must keep its local offer under review and may from time to time revise it.

(6) A local authority must from time to time publish—

(a) comments about its local offer it has received from or on behalf of—

(i) children and young people with special educational needs, and the parents of children with special educational needs, and

(ii) children and young people who have a disability, and the parents of children who have a disability, and

(b) the authority's response to those comments (including details of any action the authority intends to take).

(7) Comments published under subsection (6)(a) must be published in a form that does not enable the person making them to be identified.

(8) Regulations may make provision about—

(a) the information to be included in an authority's local offer;

(b) how an authority's local offer is to be published;

(c) who is to be consulted by an authority in preparing and reviewing its local offer;

(d) how an authority is to involve—

(i) children and young people with special educational needs, and the parents of children with special educational needs, and

(ii) children and young people who have a disability, and the parents of children who have a disability,

in the preparation and review of its local offer;

(e) the publication of comments on the local offer, and the local authority's response, under subsection (6) (including circumstances in which comments are not required to be published).

(9)The regulations may in particular require an authority's local offer to include—

(a)information about how to obtain an EHC needs assessment;

(b)information about other sources of information, advice and support for—

(i)children and young people with special educational needs and those who care for them, and

(ii)children and young people who have a disability and those who care for them;

(c)information about gaining access to provision additional to, or different from, the provision mentioned in subsection (2);

(d)information about how to make a complaint about provision mentioned in subsection (2).

31 Co-operating in specific cases: local authority functions

(1)This section applies where a local authority in England requests the cooperation of any of the following persons and bodies in the exercise of a function under this Part—

(a)another local authority;

(b)a youth offending team;

(c)the person in charge of any relevant youth accommodation;

(d)the National Health Service Commissioning Board;

(e) a clinical commissioning group;

(f) a Local Health Board;

(g)an NHS trust or NHS foundation trust.

(2)The person or body must comply with the request, unless the person or body considers that doing so would—

(a)be incompatible with the duties of the person or body, or

(b)otherwise have an adverse effect on the exercise of the functions of the person or body.

(3)A person or body that decides not to comply with a request under subsection (1) must give the authority that made the request written reasons for the decision.

(4)Regulations may provide that, where a person or body is under a duty to comply with a request to co-operate with a local authority in securing an EHC needs assessment, a detained person's EHC needs assessment or the preparation of an EHC plan, the person or body must comply with the request within a prescribed period, unless a prescribed exception applies.

32 Advice and information

(1) A local authority in England must arrange for children and young people for whom it is responsible, and the parents of children for whom it is responsible, to be provided with **advice and information** about matters relating to the special educational needs of the children or young people concerned.

Each local authority will provide a free service usually called 'sendiass' who help mediate disputes free of cost. The are sometimes ran by citizens advice. They are limited in staff so expect a few days before they initially contact you but are a good resource to help advocate and share information.

(2) A local authority in England must arrange for children and young people in its area with a disability, and the parents of children in its area with a disability, to be provided with advice and information about matters relating to the disabilities of the children or young people concerned.

(3) The authority must take such steps as it thinks appropriate for making the services provided under subsections (1) and (2) known to—

(a) the parents of children in its area;

(b) children in its area;

(c) young people in its area;

(d) the head teachers, proprietors and principals of schools and post-16 institutions in its area.

(4) The authority may also take such steps as it thinks appropriate for making the services provided under subsections (1) and (2) known to such other persons as it thinks appropriate.

Mainstream education

33 Children and young people with EHC plans

(1) This section applies where a local authority is securing the preparation of an EHC plan for a child or young person who is to be educated in a school or post-16 institution.

(2)In a case within section 39(5) or 40(2), the local authority must secure that the plan provides for the child or young person to be educated in a maintained nursery school, mainstream school or mainstream post-16 institution, unless that is incompatible with—

(a)the wishes of the child's parent or the young person, or (b)the

provision of efficient education for others.

(3) A local authority may rely on the exception in subsection (2)(b) in relation to maintained nursery schools, mainstream schools or mainstream post-16 institutions in its area taken as a whole only if it shows that there are no reasonable steps that it could take to prevent the incompatibility.

(4) A local authority may rely on the exception in subsection (2)(b) in relation to a particular maintained nursery school, mainstream school or mainstream post16 institution only if it shows that there are no reasonable steps that it or the governing body, proprietor or principal could take to prevent the incompatibility.

(5)The governing body, proprietor or principal of a maintained nursery school, mainstream school or mainstream post-16 institution may rely on the exception in subsection (2)(b) only if they show that there are no reasonable steps that they or the local authority could take to prevent the incompatibility.

(6)Subsection (2) does not prevent the child or young person from being educated in an independent school, a non-maintained special school or a special post-16 institution, if the cost is not to be met by a local authority or the Secretary of State.

(7)This section does not affect the operation of section 63 (fees payable by local authority for special educational provision at non-maintained schools and post-16 institutions).

34Children and young people with special educational needs but no EHC plan
(1)This section applies to a child or young person in England who has special educational needs but for whom no EHC plan is maintained, if he or she is to be educated in a school or post-16 institution.

(2)The child or young person must be educated in a maintained nursery school, mainstream school or mainstream post-16 institution, subject to subsections (3) and (4).

(3) The child or young person may be educated in an independent school, a nonmaintained special school or a special post-16 institution, if the cost is not to be met by a local authority or the Secretary of State.

(4) The child or young person may be educated in a special school or special post16 institution during any period in which any of subsections (5) to (9) applies.

(5) This subsection applies while the child or young person is admitted to a special school or special post-16 institution for the purposes of an EHC needs assessment, if all the following have agreed to his or her admission to the school or post-16 institution—

(a) the local authority which is responsible for him or her;

(b) the head teacher of the school or the principal of the Academy or post-16 institution;

(c) the child's parent or the young person;

(d) anyone else whose advice is required to be obtained in connection with the assessment by virtue of regulations under section 36(11).

(6) This subsection applies while the child or young person remains admitted to a special school or special post-16 institution, in prescribed circumstances, following an EHC needs assessment at the school or post-16 institution.

(7) This subsection applies while the child or young person is admitted to a special school or special post-16 institution, following a change in his or her circumstances, if all the following have agreed to his or her admission to the school or post-16 institution—

(a) the local authority which is responsible for him or her;

(b) the head teacher of the school or the principal of the Academy or post-16 institution;

(c) the child's parent or the young person.

(8) This subsection applies while the child or young person is admitted to a special school which is established in a hospital and is— (a) a community or foundation special school, or (b) an Academy school.

(9) This subsection applies while the child is admitted to a special school or special post-16 institution that is an Academy, if the Academy arrangements made in respect

of the school or post-16 institution permit it to admit children and young people with special educational needs for whom no EHC plan is maintained.

(10) This section does not affect the operation of section 63 (fees payable by local authority for special educational provision at non-maintained schools and post16 institutions).

35 Children with SEN in maintained nurseries and mainstream schools

(1) This section applies where a child with special educational needs is being educated in a maintained nursery school or a mainstream school.

(2) Those concerned with making special educational provision for the child must secure that the child engages in the activities of the school together with children who do not have special educational needs, subject to subsection (3).

(3) Subsection (2) applies only so far as is reasonably practicable **and is compatible with—**

(a) the child receiving the special educational provision called for by his or her special educational needs,

(b) the provision of efficient education for the children with whom he or she will be educated, and

(c) the efficient use of resources.

This section is the response a school might give for not allowing your child to attend their school. It may be that they are simply 'full' but by law this cannot be used as a reason and so the above statements are used. This is a national shortage of places in Special Schools in 204 so this is often the response school give who are already over subscribed.

Assessment

36 Assessment of education, health and care needs

(1) A request for a local authority in England to secure an EHC needs assessment for a child or young person may be made to the authority by the child's parent, the young person or a person acting on behalf of a school or post-16 institution.

(2) An "EHC needs assessment" is an assessment of the educational, health care and social care needs of a child or young person.

(3) When a request is made to a local authority under subsection (1), or a local authority otherwise becomes responsible for a child or young person, the authority must determine whether it may be necessary for special educational provision to be made for the child or young person in accordance with an EHC plan.

(4) In making a determination under subsection (3), the local authority must consult the child's parent or the young person.

(5) Where the local authority determines that it is not necessary for special educational provision to be made for the child or young person in accordance with an EHC plan it must notify the child's parent or the young person—

(a) of the reasons for that determination, and

(b) that accordingly it has decided not to secure an EHC needs assessment for the child or young person.

(6) Subsection (7) applies where—

(a) no EHC plan is maintained for the child or young person,

(b) the child or young person has not been assessed under this section or section 71 during the previous six months, and

(c) the local authority determines that it may be necessary for special educational provision to be made for the child or young person in accordance with an EHC plan.

(7) The authority must notify the child's parent or the young person—

(a) that it is considering securing an EHC needs assessment for the child or young person, and

(b) that the parent or young person has the right to— (i) express views to the authority (orally or in writing), and (ii) submit evidence to the authority.

(8) The local authority must secure an EHC needs assessment for the child or young person if, after having regard to any views expressed and evidence submitted under subsection (7), the authority is of the opinion that— (a) the child or young person has or may have special educational needs, and

(b) it may be necessary for special educational provision to be made for the child or young person in accordance with an EHC plan.

If you secure a needs assessment i.e an EHCPA this doesn't guarantee it will become a EHCP at the end of the 6 weeks. Please note due to a national shortage of educational psychologists required to carry out an assessment there are delays to this up to 52 weeks ! – (2024 data) however this back log is starting to reduce down to 6 months.

(9)After an EHC needs assessment has been carried out, the local authority must notify the child's parent or the young person of—

(a)the outcome of the assessment,

(b)whether it proposes to secure that an EHC plan is prepared for the child or young person, and

(c)the reasons for that decision.

(10)In making a determination or forming an opinion for the purposes of this section in relation to a young person aged over 18, a local authority must consider whether he or she requires additional time, in comparison to the majority of others of the same age who do not have special educational needs, to complete his or her education or training.

(11)Regulations may make provision about EHC needs assessments, in particular—

(a)about requests under subsection (1);

(b)imposing time limits in relation to consultation under subsection (4);

(c)about giving notice;

(d)about expressing views and submitting evidence under subsection (7);

(e)about how assessments are to be conducted;

(f)about advice to be obtained in connection with an assessment;

(g)about combining an EHC needs assessment with other assessments;

(h)about the use for the purposes of an EHC needs assessment of information obtained as a result of other assessments;

(i)about the use of information obtained as a result of an EHC needs assessment, including the use of that information for the purposes of other assessments;

(j)about the provision of information, advice and support in connection with an EHC needs assessment.

Education, health and care plans

37 Education, health and care plans

(1) Where, in the light of an EHC needs assessment, it is necessary for special educational provision to be made for a child or young person in accordance with an EHC plan—

(a) the local authority must secure that an EHC plan is prepared for the child or young person, and

(b) once an EHC plan has been prepared, it must maintain the plan.

(2) For the purposes of this Part, an EHC plan is a plan specifying—

(a) the child's or young person's special educational needs;

(b) the outcomes sought for him or her;

(c) the special educational provision required by him or her;

(d) any health care provision reasonably required by the learning difficulties and disabilities which result in him or her having special educational needs;

(e) in the case of a child or a young person aged under 18, any social care provision which must be made for him or her by the local authority as a result of section 2 of the Chronically Sick and Disabled Persons Act 1970 (as it applies by virtue of section 28A of that Act);

(f) any social care provision reasonably required by the learning difficulties and disabilities which result in the child or young person having special educational needs, to the extent that the provision is not already specified in the plan under paragraph (e).

(3) An EHC plan may also specify other health care and social care provision reasonably required by the child or young person.

(4) Regulations may make provision about the preparation, content, maintenance, amendment and disclosure of EHC plans.

(5) Regulations under subsection (4) about amendments of EHC plans must include provision applying section 33 (mainstream education for children and young people with EHC plans) to a case where an EHC plan is to be amended under those regulations.

38 Preparation of EHC plans: draft plan

(1) Where a local authority is required to secure that an EHC plan is prepared for a child or young person, it must consult the child's parent or the young person

about the content of the plan during the preparation of a draft of the plan.

(2)The local authority must then—

(a)send the draft plan to the child's parent or the young person, and

(b)give the parent or young person notice of his or her right to— (i)make representations about the content of the draft plan, and

(ii)request the authority to secure that a particular school or other institution within subsection (3) is named in the plan.

(3)A school or other institution is within this subsection if it is—

(a)   a maintained school;
(b)   a maintained nursery school;
(c)an Academy;

(d)an institution within the further education sector in England;

(e)a non-maintained special school;

(f)an institution approved by the Secretary of State under section 41 (independent special schools and special post-16 institutions: approval).

(4)A notice under subsection (2)(b) must specify a period before the end of which any representations or requests must be made.

(5)The draft EHC plan sent to the child's parent or the young person must not—

(a)name a school or other institution, or

(b)specify a type of school or other institution.

39Finalising EHC plans: request for particular school or other institution
(1)This section applies where, before the end of the period specified in a notice under section 38(2)(b), a request is made to a local authority to secure that a particular school or other institution is named in an EHC plan.

(2)The local authority must consult—

(a)the governing body, proprietor or principal of the school or other institution,

(b)the governing body, proprietor or principal of any other school or other institution the authority is considering having named in the plan, and

(c) if a school or other institution is within paragraph (a) or (b) and is maintained by another local authority, that authority.

(3) The local authority must secure that the EHC plan names the school or other institution specified in the request, unless subsection (4) applies.

(4) This subsection applies where—

(a) the school or other institution requested is unsuitable for the age, ability, aptitude or special educational needs of the child or young person concerned, or

(b) the attendance of the child or young person at the requested school or other institution would be incompatible with—

(i) the provision of efficient education for others, or (ii) the

efficient use of resources.

(5) Where subsection (4) applies, the local authority must secure that the plan—
(a) names a school or other institution which the local authority thinks would be appropriate for the child or young person, or

(b) specifies the type of school or other institution which the local authority thinks would be appropriate for the child or young person.

(6) Before securing that the plan names a school or other institution under subsection (5)(a), the local authority must (if it has not already done so) consult—

(a) the governing body, proprietor or principal of any school or other institution the authority is considering having named in the plan, and

(b) if that school or other institution is maintained by another local authority, that authority.

(7) The local authority must, at the end of the period specified in the notice under section 38(2)(b), secure that any changes it thinks necessary are made to the draft EHC plan.

(8) The local authority must send a copy of the finalised EHC plan to—

(a) the child's parent or the young person, and

(b) the governing body, proprietor or principal of any school or other institution named in the plan.

40 Finalising EHC plans: no request for particular school or other institution (1) This section applies where no request is made to a local authority before the end of the

period specified in a notice under section 38(2)(b) to secure that a particular school or other institution is named in an EHC plan.

(2)The local authority must secure that the plan—

(a)names a school or other institution which the local authority thinks would be appropriate for the child or young person concerned, or

(b)specifies the type of school or other institution which the local authority thinks would be appropriate for the child or young person.

(3)Before securing that the plan names a school or other institution under subsection (2)(a), the local authority must consult—

(a)the governing body, proprietor or principal of any school or other institution the authority is considering having named in the plan, and

(b)if that school or other institution is maintained by another local authority, that authority.

(4)The local authority must also secure that any changes it thinks necessary are made to the draft EHC plan.

(5)The local authority must send a copy of the finalised EHC plan to—

(a)the child's parent or the young person, and

(b)the governing body, proprietor or principal of any school or other institution named in the plan.

41Independent special schools and special post-16 institutions: approval

(1)The Secretary of State may approve an institution within subsection (2) for the purpose of enabling the institution to be the subject of a request for it to be named in an EHC plan.

(2)An institution is within this subsection if it is—

(a)an independent educational institution (within the meaning of Chapter 1 of Part 4 of ESA 2008)—

(i)which has been entered on the register of independent educational institutions in England (kept under section 95 of that Act), and

(ii)which is specially organised to make special educational provision for students with special educational needs,

(b)an independent school—

(i)which has been entered on the register of independent schools in Wales (kept under section 158 of the Education Act 2002), and

(ii)which is specially organised to make special educational provision for pupils with special educational needs, or

(c)a special post-16 institution which is not an institution within the further education sector or a 16 to 19 Academy.

(3)The Secretary of State may approve an institution under subsection (1) only if its proprietor consents.

(4)The Secretary of State may withdraw approval given under subsection (1).

(5)Regulations may make provision about giving and withdrawing approval under this section, in particular—

(a)about the types of special post-16 institutions which may be approved under subsection (1);

(b)specifying criteria which an institution must meet before it can be approved under subsection (1);

(c)about the matters which may or must be taken into account in deciding to give or withdraw approval;

(d)about the publication of a list of all institutions who are approved under this section.

42 Duty to secure special educational provision and health care provision in accordance with EHC Plan

(1)This section applies where a local authority maintains an EHC plan for a child or young person.

(2)The local authority must secure the specified special educational provision for the child or young person.

(3)If the plan specifies health care provision, the responsible commissioning body must arrange the specified health care provision for the child or young person.

(4)"The responsible commissioning body", in relation to any specified health care provision, means the body (or each body) that is under a duty to arrange health care provision of that kind in respect of the child or young person.

(5)Subsections (2) and (3) do not apply if the child's parent or the young person has made suitable alternative arrangements.

(6) "Specified", in relation to an EHC plan, means specified in the plan.

43 Schools and other institutions named in EHC plan: duty to admit

(1) Subsection (2) applies if one of the following is named in an EHC plan—

(a) a maintained school;

(b) a maintained nursery school;

(c) an Academy;

(d) an institution within the further education sector in England;

(e) a non-maintained special school;

(f) an institution approved by the Secretary of State under section 41.

(2) The governing body, proprietor or principal of the school or other institution must admit the child or young person for whom the plan is maintained.

(3) Subsection (2) has effect regardless of any duty imposed on the governing body of a school by section 1(6) of SSFA 1998.

(4) Subsection (2) does not affect any power to exclude a pupil or student from a school or other institution.

44 Reviews and re-assessments

(1) A local authority must review an EHC plan that it maintains—

(a) in the period of 12 months starting with the date on which the plan was first made, and

(b) in each subsequent period of 12 months starting with the date on which the plan was last reviewed under this section.

(2) A local authority must secure a re-assessment of the educational, health care and social care needs of a child or young person for whom it maintains an EHC plan if a request is made to it by—

(a) the child's parent or the young person, or

(b) the governing body, proprietor or principal of the school, post-16 institution or other institution which the child or young person attends.

(3) A local authority may also secure a re-assessment of those needs at any other time if it thinks it necessary.

(4) Subsections (1) and (2) are subject to any contrary provision in regulations made under subsection (7)(b).

(5) In reviewing an EHC plan maintained for a young person aged over 18, or deciding whether to secure a re-assessment of the needs of such a young person, a local authority must have regard to whether the educational or training outcomes specified in the plan have been achieved.

(6) During a review or re-assessment, a local authority must consult the parent of the child, or the young person, for whom it maintains the EHC plan.

(7) Regulations may make provision about reviews and re-assessments, in particular—

(a) about other circumstances in which a local authority must or may review an EHC plan or secure a re-assessment (including before the end of a specified phase of a child's or young person's education);

(b) about circumstances in which it is not necessary for a local authority to review an EHC plan or secure a re-assessment;

(c) about amending or replacing an EHC plan following a review or re-assessment.

(8) Regulations under subsection (7) about re-assessments may in particular apply provisions of or made under this Part that are applicable to EHC needs assessments, with or without modifications.

(9) Regulations under subsection (7)(c) must include provision applying section 33 (mainstream education for children and young people with EHC plans) to a case where an EHC plan is to be amended following a review.

45 Ceasing to maintain an EHC plan

(1) A local authority may cease to maintain an EHC plan for a child or young person only if—

(a) the authority is no longer responsible for the child or young person, or

(b) the authority determines that it is no longer necessary for the plan to be maintained.

(2) The circumstances in which it is no longer necessary for an EHC plan to be maintained for a child or young person include where the child or young person no longer requires the special educational provision specified in the plan.

(3) When determining whether a young person aged over 18 no longer requires the special educational provision specified in his or her EHC plan, a local authority must

have regard to whether the educational or training outcomes specified in the plan have been achieved.

(4)A local authority may not cease to maintain an EHC plan for a child or young person until—

(a)after the end of the period allowed for bringing an appeal under section 51 against its decision to cease to maintain the plan, where no such appeal is brought before the end of that period;

(b)after the appeal has been finally determined, where such an appeal is brought before the end of that period.

(5)Regulations may make provision about ceasing to maintain an EHC plan, in particular about—

(a)other circumstances in which it is no longer necessary for an EHC plan to be maintained;

(b)circumstances in which a local authority may not determine that it is no longer necessary for an EHC plan to be maintained;

(c)the procedure to be followed by a local authority when determining whether to cease to maintain an EHC plan.

46 Maintaining an EHC plan after young person's 25th birthday

(1)A local authority may continue to maintain an EHC plan for a young person until the end of the academic year during which the young person attains the age of 25.

(2)"Academic year" means the period of twelve months ending on the prescribed date.

47 Transfer of EHC plans

(1)Regulations may make provision for an EHC plan maintained for a child or young person by one local authority to be transferred to another local authority in England, where the other authority becomes responsible for the child or young person.

(2)The regulations may in particular—

(a)impose a duty on the other authority to maintain the plan;

(b)treat the plan as if originally prepared by the other authority;

(c)treat things done by the transferring authority in relation to the plan as done by the other authority.

48 Release of child or young person for whom EHC plan previously maintained

(1) This section applies where—

(a) a child or young person who has been subject to a detention order (within the meaning of section 562(1A)(a) of EA 1996) is released,

(b) on the release date, a local authority in England becomes responsible for him or her, and

(c) an EHC plan was—

(i) maintained for him or her immediately before the start of the detention, or (ii) kept

for him or her under section 74 during the detention.

(2) The local authority must—

(a) maintain the plan, and

(b) review the plan as soon as reasonably practicable after the release date.

(3) Subsection (2)(b) is subject to any contrary provision in regulations under section 44(7)(b).

49 Personal budgets and direct payments

(1) A local authority that maintains an EHC plan, or is securing the preparation of an EHC plan, for a child or young person must prepare a personal budget for him or her if asked to do so by the child's parent or the young person.

(2) The authority prepares a "personal budget" for the child or young person if it identifies an amount as available to secure particular provision that is specified, or proposed to be specified, in the EHC plan, with a view to the child's parent or the young person being involved in securing the provision.

(3) Regulations may make provision about personal budgets, in particular—

(a) about requests for personal budgets;

(b) about the amount of a personal budget;

(c) about the sources of the funds making up a personal budget;

(d) for payments ("direct payments") representing all or part of a personal budget to be made to a child's parent or a young person, or a person of a prescribed description in prescribed circumstances, in order to secure provision to which the budget relates;

(e) about the description of provision to which personal budgets and direct payments may (and may not) relate;

(f) for a personal budget or direct payment to cover the agreed cost of the provision to which the budget or payment relates;

(g) about when, how, to whom and on what conditions direct payments may (and may not) be made;

(h) about when direct payments may be required to be repaid and the recovery of unpaid sums;

(i) about conditions with which a person or body making direct payments must comply before, after or at the time of making a direct payment;

(j) about arrangements for providing information, advice or support in connection with personal budgets and direct payments.

(4) If the regulations include provision authorising direct payments, they must—

(a) require the consent of a child's parent or a young person, or a person of a prescribed description in prescribed circumstances, to be obtained before direct payments are made;

(b) require the authority to stop making direct payments where the required consent is withdrawn.

(5) Special educational provision acquired by means of a direct payment made by a

local authority is to be treated as having been secured by the authority in pursuance of its duty under section 42(2), subject to any prescribed conditions or exceptions.

(6) Subsection (7) applies if—

(a) an EHC plan is maintained for a child or young person, and

(b) health care provision specified in the plan is acquired for him or her by means of a payment made by a commissioning body under section 12A(1) of the National Health Service Act 2006 (direct payments for health care).

(7) The health care provision is to be treated as having been arranged by the commissioning body in pursuance of its duty under section 42(3) of this Act, subject to any prescribed conditions or exceptions.

(8) "Commissioning body", in relation to any specified health care provision, means a body that is under a duty to arrange health care provision of that kind in respect of the child or young person.

50 Continuation of services under section 17 of the Children Act 1989

After section 17 of the Children Act 1989 (provision of services for children etc) insert—

"17ZG Section 17 services: continued provision where EHC plan maintained (1) This section applies where, immediately before a child in need reaches the age of 18—

(a) a local authority in England is providing services for the child in the exercise of functions conferred by section 17, and

(b) an EHC plan is maintained for the child.

(2) The local authority may continue to provide services for the child in the exercise of those functions after the child reaches the age of 18, but may not continue to do so after the EHC plan has ceased to be maintained.

(3) In this section "EHC plan" means a plan within section 37(2) of the Children and Families Act 2014."

Appeals, mediation and dispute resolution

51 Appeals

Below is a list of common reasons parents and carers appeal EHCPs . The letter sent will have all the appeals process details on there. Use it, its free and will follow the proper processes and go back to panel.

(1) A child's parent or a young person may appeal to the First-tier Tribunal against the matters set out in subsection (2), subject to section 55 (mediation).

(2) The matters are—

(a)   a decision of a local authority not to secure an EHC needs assessment for the child or young person;

(b)   a decision of a local authority, following an EHC needs assessment, that it is not necessary for special educational provision to be made for the child or young person in accordance with an EHC plan;

(c) where an EHC plan is maintained for the child or young person—

(i) the child's or young person's special educational needs as specified in the plan;

(ii) the special educational provision specified in the plan;

(iii)the school or other institution named in the plan, or the type of school or other institution specified in the plan;

(iv)if no school or other institution is named in the plan, that fact;

(d) a decision of a local authority not to secure a re-assessment of the needs of the child or young person under section 44 following a request to do so;

(e) a decision of a local authority not to secure the amendment or replacement of an EHC plan it maintains for the child or young person following a review or reassessment under section 44;

(f) a decision of a local authority under section 45 to cease to maintain an EHC plan for the child or young person.

(3)A child's parent or a young person may appeal to the First-tier Tribunal under subsection (2)(c)—

(a)when an EHC plan is first finalised for the child or young person, and (b)following an amendment or replacement of the plan. – wait for it to be finalised! you cant appeal the draft version !

(4)Regulations may make provision about appeals to the First-tier Tribunal in respect of EHC needs assessments and EHC plans, in particular about— (a)other matters relating to EHC plans against which appeals may be brought;

(b)making and determining appeals;

(c)the powers of the First-tier Tribunal on determining an appeal; (d)unopposed appeals.

(5)Regulations under subsection (4)(c) may include provision conferring power on the First-tier Tribunal, on determining an appeal against a matter, to make recommendations in respect of other matters (including matters against which no appeal may be brought).

(6) A person commits an offence if without reasonable excuse that person fails to comply with any requirement—

(a)in respect of the discovery or inspection of documents, or (b)to

attend to give evidence and produce documents,

where that requirement is imposed by Tribunal Procedure Rules in relation to an appeal under this section or regulations under subsection (4)(a).

(7)   A person guilty of an offence under subsection (6) is liable on summary conviction to a fine not exceeding level 3 on the standard scale.

52 Right to mediation

(1)This section applies where—

(a)a decision against which an appeal may be brought under section 51 is made in respect of a child or young person, or

(b)an EHC plan for a child or young person is made, amended or replaced.

(2)Before the end of the prescribed period after the decision is made, or the plan is made, amended or replaced, the local authority must notify the child's parent or the young person of—

(a)the right to mediation under section 53 or 54, and

(b)the requirement to obtain a certificate under section 55 before making certain appeals.

(3)If the parent or young person wishes to pursue mediation under section 53 or 54, he or she must inform the local authority of—

(a)that fact, and

(b)the issues in respect of which he or she wishes to pursue mediation ("the mediation issues").

(4)If the mediation issues are, or include, the fact that no health care provision, or no health care provision of a particular kind, is specified in the plan, the parent or young person must also inform the local authority of the health care provision which he or she wishes to be specified in the plan.

53 Mediation: health care issues

(1)This section applies where—

(a)the parent or young person informs the local authority under section 52 that he or she wishes to pursue mediation, and (b)the mediation issues include health care provision specified in the plan or the fact that no health care provision, or no health care provision of a particular kind, is specified in the plan.

(2)The local authority must notify each relevant commissioning body of—

(a)the mediation issues, and

(b)anything of which it has been informed by the parent or young person under section 52(4).

(3)If the mediation issues are limited to the health care provision specified in the plan or the fact that no health care provision, or no health care provision of a particular kind, is specified in the plan, the responsible commissioning body (or, where there is more than one, the responsible commissioning bodies acting jointly) must—
(a)arrange for mediation between it (or them) and the parent or young person,

(b)ensure that the mediation is conducted by an independent person, and

(c)participate in the mediation.

(4)If the mediation issues include anything else—

(a)the local authority must—

(i)arrange for mediation between it, each responsible commissioning body and the parent or young person,

(ii)ensure that the mediation is conducted by an independent person, and

(iii)participate in the mediation, and

(b)each responsible commissioning body must also participate in the mediation.

(5)For the purposes of this section, a person is not independent if he or she is employed by any of the following— (a)a local authority in England;

(b)a clinical commissioning group;

(c)the National Health Service Commissioning Board.

(6)In this section "responsible commissioning body"—

(a)if the mediation issues in question are or include the health care provision specified in an EHC plan, means a body that is under a duty to arrange health care provision of that kind in respect of the child or young person;

(b)if the mediation issues in question are or include the fact that no health care provision, or no health care provision of a particular kind, is specified in an EHC plan, means a body that would be under a duty to arrange health care provision of the kind in question if it were specified in the plan.

54 Mediation: educational and social care issues etc

(1)This section applies where—

(a)the parent or young person informs the local authority under section 52 that he or she wishes to pursue mediation, and

(b)the mediation issues do not include health care provision specified in the plan or the fact that no health care provision, or no health care provision of a particular kind, is specified in the plan.

(2)The local authority must—

(a)arrange for mediation between it and the parent or young person, (b)ensure that the mediation is conducted by an independent person, and (c)participate in the mediation.

(3)For the purposes of this section, a person is not independent if he or she is employed by a local authority in England.

55 Mediation

(1)This section applies where a child's parent or young person intends to appeal to the First-tier Tribunal under section 51 or regulations made under that section in respect of—

(a)a decision of a local authority, or

(b)the content of an EHC plan maintained by a local authority.

(2)But this section does not apply in respect of an appeal concerning only—

(a)the school or other institution named in an EHC plan;

(b)the type of school or other institution specified in an EHC plan;

(c)the fact that an EHC plan does not name a school or other institution.

(3)The parent or young person may make the appeal only if a mediation adviser has issued a certificate to him or her under subsection (4) or (5).

(4) A mediation adviser must issue a certificate under this subsection to the parent or young person if—

(a)the adviser has provided him or her with information and advice about pursuing mediation under section 53 or 54, and

(b)the parent or young person has informed the adviser that he or she does not wish to pursue mediation.

(5) A mediation adviser must issue a certificate under this subsection to the parent or young person if the adviser has provided him or her with information and advice about pursuing mediation under section 53 or 54, and the parent or young person has—

(6) MAKE SURE YOU GET YOUR MEDIATION CERTIFICATE

(a)informed the adviser that he or she wishes to pursue mediation under the appropriate section, and

(b)participated in such mediation.

56Mediation: supplementary
(1)Regulations may make provision for the purposes of sections 52 to 55, in particular—

(a)about giving notice;

(b)imposing time limits;

(c)enabling a local authority or commissioning body to take prescribed steps following the conclusion of mediation;

(d)about who may attend mediation;

(e)where a child's parent is a party to mediation, requiring the mediator to take reasonable steps to ascertain the views of the child;

(f)about the provision of advocacy and other support services for the parent or young person;

(g)requiring a local authority or commissioning body to pay reasonable travel expenses and other expenses of a prescribed description, up to any prescribed limit;

(h)about exceptions to the requirement in section 55(3);

(i)about the training, qualifications and experience of mediators and mediation advisers;

(j)conferring powers or imposing requirements on local authorities, commissioning bodies, mediators and mediation advisers.

(2)In section 55 and this section "mediation adviser" means an independent person who can provide information and advice about pursuing mediation.

(3)For the purposes of subsection (2), a person is not independent if he or she is employed by any of the following— (a)a local authority in England;

(b)a clinical commissioning group;

(c)the National Health Service Commissioning Board.

(4)In this section "commissioning body" means a body that is under a duty to arrange health care provision of any kind.

57 Resolution of disagreements

(1)A local authority in England must make arrangements with a view to avoiding or resolving disagreements within subsection (2) or (3).

(2)The disagreements within this subsection are those about the exercise by the local authority or relevant bodies of their functions under this Part, where the disagreement is between—

(a)the local authority or a relevant body, and

(b)the parents of children, and young people, in the authority's area.

(3)The disagreements within this subsection are those about the exercise by the local authority of its functions relating to EHC needs assessments, the preparation and review of EHC plans, and re-assessment of educational, health care and social care needs, where the disagreement is between—

(a)the local authority and a responsible commissioning body, or

(b)a responsible commissioning body and the parents of children, or young people, in the authority's area.

(4)A local authority in England must make arrangements with a view to avoiding or resolving, in each relevant school or post-16 institution, disagreements within subsection (5).

(5)The disagreements within this subsection are those about the special educational provision made for a child or young person with special educational needs who is a registered pupil or a student at the relevant school or post-16 institution concerned, where the disagreement is between—

(a)the child's parent, or the young person, and

(b)the appropriate authority for the school or post-16 institution.

(6)Arrangements within this section must provide for the appointment of independent persons with the function of facilitating the avoidance or resolution of the disagreements to which the arrangements apply.

(7)For the purposes of subsection (6) a person is not independent if he or she is employed by any of the following— (a)a local authority in England;

(b)a clinical commissioning group;

(c)the National Health Service Commissioning Board.

(8) A local authority in England must take such steps as it thinks appropriate for making the arrangements under this section known to—

(a)the parents of children in its area with special educational needs,

(b)young people in its area with special educational needs, and

(c)the head teachers, governing bodies, proprietors and principals of schools and post-16 institutions in its area.

(9) A local authority in England may take such steps as it thinks appropriate for making the arrangements under this section known to such other persons as it thinks appropriate.

(10)In this section—

- "relevant body" means—

    (a) the governing body of a maintained school, maintained nursery school or institution within the further education sector;

    (b) the proprietor of an Academy;

- "relevant school or post-16 institution" means—
  - (a) a maintained school;
  - (b) a maintained nursery school;
  - (c) a post-16 institution;
  - (d) an Academy;
  - (e) an independent school;
  - (f) a non-maintained special school;
  - (g) a pupil referral unit;
  - (h) a place at which relevant early years education is provided;
- "responsible commissioning body", in relation to any particular health care provision, means a body that is under a duty to arrange health care provision of that kind in respect of the child or young person concerned.

(11) For the purposes of this section, the "appropriate authority" for a relevant school or post-16 institution is—

(a) in the case of a maintained school, maintained nursery school or nonmaintained special school, the governing body;

(b) in the case of a post-16 institution, the governing body, proprietor or principal;

(c) in the case of an Academy or independent school, the proprietor;

(d) in the case of a pupil referral unit, the management committee;

(e) in the case of a place at which relevant early years education is provided, the provider of the relevant early years education.

58 Appeals and claims by children: pilot schemes

(1)The Secretary of State may by order make pilot schemes enabling children in England to—

(a)appeal to the First-tier Tribunal under section 51;

(b)make a claim to the First-tier Tribunal under Schedule 17 to the Equality Act 2010 (disabled pupils: enforcement) that a responsible body in England has contravened Chapter 1 of Part 6 of that Act because of the child's disability.

(2)An order under subsection (1) may, in particular, make provision—

(a)about the age from which children may appeal or make a claim;

(b)in respect of appeals under section 51, about mediation and the application of section 55;

(c)about the bringing of appeals or making of claims by a child and by his or her parent concurrently;

(d)about determining whether a child is capable of bringing an appeal or making a claim, and the assistance and support a child may require to be able to do so;

(e)enabling a person to exercise a child's rights under an order under subsection (1) on behalf of the child;

(f)enabling children to have access to advice and information which is available to a parent or young person in respect of an appeal or claim of a kind mentioned in subsection (1);

(g)about the provision of advocacy and other support services to children;

(h)requiring notices to be given to a child (as well as to his or her parent);

(i)requiring documents to be served on a child (as well as on his or her parent).

(3)An order under subsection (1) may apply a statutory provision, with or without modifications.

(4)In subsection (3), "statutory provision" means a provision made by or under this or any other Act, whenever passed or made.

(5)This section is repealed at the end of five years beginning with the day on which this Act is passed.

59Appeals and claims by children: follow-up provision

(1)The Secretary of State may by order provide that children in England may—

(a)appeal to the First-tier Tribunal under section 51;

(b)make a claim to the First-tier Tribunal under Schedule 17 to the Equality Act 2010 (disabled pupils: enforcement) that a responsible body in England has contravened Chapter 1 of Part 6 of that Act because of the child's disability.

(2)The Secretary of State may not make an order under subsection (1) until the end of two years beginning with the day on which the first order is made under section 58(1).

(3)An order under subsection (1) may, in particular, make provision—

(a)about the age from which children may appeal or make a claim;

(b)in respect of appeals under section 51, about mediation and the application of section 55;

(c)about the bringing of appeals or making of claims by a child and by his or her parent concurrently;

(d)about determining whether a child is capable of bringing an appeal or making a claim, and the assistance and support a child may require to be able to do so;

(e)enabling a person to exercise a child's rights under an order under subsection (1) on behalf of the child;

(f)enabling children to have access to advice and information which is available to a parent or young person in respect of an appeal or claim of a kind mentioned in subsection (1);

(g)about the provision of advocacy and other support services to children;

(h)requiring notices to be given to a child (as well as to his or her parent);

(i)requiring documents to be served on a child (as well as on his or her parent).

(4)An order under subsection (1) may—

(a)amend, repeal or revoke a statutory provision, or

(b)apply a statutory provision, with or without modifications.

(5)In subsection (4), "statutory provision" means a provision made by or under this or any other Act, whenever passed or made.

60Equality Act 2010: claims against schools by disabled young people

In Part 2 of Schedule 17 to the Equality Act 2010 (disabled pupils: enforcement in tribunals in England and Wales), in paragraph 3 (who may make a claim that a school has contravened Chapter 1 of Part 6 of that Act because of a person's disability) for "to the Tribunal by the person's parent" substitute "—

(a) to the English Tribunal by the person's parent or, if the person is over compulsory school age, the person;

(b) to the Welsh Tribunal by the person's parent."

Special educational provision: functions of local authorities

61 Special educational provision otherwise than in schools, post-16 institutions etc

(1) A local authority in England may arrange for any special educational provision that it has decided is necessary for a child or young person for whom it is responsible to be made otherwise than in a school or post-16 institution or a place at which relevant early years education is provided.

(2) An authority may do so only if satisfied that it would be inappropriate for the provision to be made in a school or post-16 institution or at such a place.

(3) Before doing so, the authority must consult the child's parent or the young person.

62 Special educational provision outside England and Wales

(1) This section applies where a local authority in England makes arrangements for a child or young person for whom it maintains an EHC plan to attend an institution outside England and Wales which specialises in providing for children or young people with special educational needs.

(2) The arrangements may (in particular) include contributing to or paying—

(a) fees charged by the institution;

(b) the child's or young person's travelling expenses;

(c) expenses reasonably incurred in maintaining the child or young person while at the institution or travelling to or from it;

(d) expenses reasonably incurred by someone accompanying the child or young person while travelling to or from the institution or staying there.

63 Fees for special educational provision at non-maintained schools and post-16 institutions

(1) Subsection (2) applies where—

(a) a local authority maintains an EHC plan for a child or young person,

(b) special educational provision in respect of the child or young person is made at a school, post-16 institution or place at which relevant early years education is provided, and

(c) that school, institution or place is named in the EHC plan.

(2) The local authority must pay any fees payable in respect of education or training provided for the child or young person at that school, institution or place in accordance with the EHC plan.

(3) Subsection (4) applies where—

(a) a local authority is responsible for a child or young person for whom no EHC plan is maintained,

(b) special educational provision in respect of the child or young person is made at a school, post-16 institution or place at which relevant early years education is provided, and

(c) the local authority is satisfied that—

(i) the interests of the child or young person require special educational provision to be made, and

(ii) it is appropriate for education or training to be provided to the child or young person at the school, institution or place in question.

(4) The local authority must pay any fees payable in respect of the special educational provision made at the school, institution or place in question which is required to meet the special educational needs of the child or young person.

(5) Where board and lodging are provided for the child or young person at the school, post-16 institution or place mentioned in subsection (2) or (4), the authority must also pay any fees in respect of the board and lodging, if satisfied that special educational provision cannot be provided at the school, post-16 institution or place unless the board and lodging are also provided.

64 Supply of goods and services

(1) A local authority in England may supply goods and services to—

(a) the governing body of a maintained school or maintained nursery school in England;

(b) the proprietor of an Academy;

(c) the governing body of an institution within the further education sector that the authority thinks is or is to be attended by a young person for whom the authority maintains an EHC plan, but only for the purpose set out in subsection (2).

(2)The purpose is that of assisting the governing body or proprietor in the performance of—

(a)any duty imposed on the body under section 66(2) (duty to use best endeavours to secure special educational provision called for by special educational needs);

(b)in the case of a governing body of a community or foundation special school, any duty imposed on the body.

(3)The goods and services may be supplied on the terms and conditions that the authority thinks fit, including terms as to payment.

(4)A local authority in England may supply goods and services to any authority or other person (other than a governing body or proprietor within subsection (1)), but only for the purpose set out in subsection (5).

(5)The purpose is that of assisting the authority or other person in making special educational provision for a child who is receiving relevant early years education, in a case where the authority has decided that the special educational provision is necessary for the child.

65Access to schools, post-16 institutions and other institutions

(1)This section applies where a local authority in England maintains an EHC plan for a child or young person.

(2)A person authorised by the authority is entitled to have access at any reasonable time to the premises of a school, post-16 institution or other institution at which education or training is provided in pursuance of the plan, for the purpose of monitoring the education or training.

(3)Subsection (2) does not apply to the premises of a mainstream post-16 institution in Wales.

Special educational provision: functions of governing bodies and others

66Using best endeavours to secure special educational provision

(1)This section imposes duties on the appropriate authorities for the following schools and other institutions in England—

(a)mainstream schools;

(b)maintained nursery schools;

(c)16 to 19 Academies;

(d)alternative provision Academies;

(e)institutions within the further education sector; (f)pupil referral units.

(2)If a registered pupil or a student at a school or other institution has special educational needs, the appropriate authority must, in exercising its functions in relation to the school or other institution, use its best endeavours to secure that the special educational provision called for by the pupil's or student's special educational needs is made.

(3)The "appropriate authority" for a school or other institution is—

(a)in the case of a maintained school, maintained nursery school or institution within the further education sector, the governing body;

(b)in the case of an Academy, the proprietor;

(c)in the case of a pupil referral unit, the management committee.

67 SEN co-ordinators

(1)This section imposes duties on the appropriate authorities of the following schools in England— (a)mainstream schools;

(b)maintained nursery schools.

(2)The appropriate authority must designate a member of staff at the school (to be known as the "SEN co-ordinator") as having responsibility for co-ordinating the provision for pupils with special educational needs.

(3)Regulations may—

(a)require appropriate authorities which are subject to the duty imposed by subsection (2) to ensure that SEN co-ordinators have prescribed qualifications or prescribed experience (or both);

(b)confer other functions relating to SEN co-ordinators on appropriate authorities which are subject to the duty imposed by subsection (2).

(4)The "appropriate authority" for a school is—

(a)in the case of a maintained school or maintained nursery school, the governing body;

(b)in the case of an Academy, the proprietor.

68 Informing parents and young people

(1)This section applies if—

(a) special educational provision is made for a child or young person at a maintained school, a maintained nursery school, an Academy school, an alternative provision Academy or a pupil referral unit, and

(b) no EHC plan is maintained for the child or young person.

(2) The appropriate authority for the school must inform the child's parent or the young person that special educational provision is being made for the child or young person.

(3) The "appropriate authority" for a school is—

(a) in the case of a maintained school or maintained nursery school, the governing body;

(b) in the case of an Academy school or an alternative provision Academy, the proprietor;

(c) in the case of a pupil referral unit, the management committee.

69 SEN information report

(1) This section imposes a duty on—

(a) the governing bodies of maintained schools and maintained nursery schools in England, and

(b) the proprietors of Academy schools.

(2) A governing body or proprietor must prepare a report containing SEN information.

(3) "SEN information" is—

(a) such information as may be prescribed about the implementation of the governing body's or proprietor's policy for pupils at the school with special educational needs;

(b) information as to—

(i) the arrangements for the admission of disabled persons as pupils at the school;
(ii) the steps taken to prevent disabled pupils from being treated less favourably than other pupils;

(iii) the facilities provided to assist access to the school by disabled pupils;

(iv) the plan prepared by the governing body or proprietor under paragraph 3 of Schedule 10 to the Equality Act 2010 (accessibility plan).

(4) In this section—

- "disabled person" means a person who is a disabled person for the purposes of the Equality Act 2010;

- "disabled pupil" includes a disabled person who may be admitted to a school as a pupil.

Detained persons

70 Application of Part to detained persons

(1) Subject to this section and sections 71 to 75, nothing in or made under this Part applies to, or in relation to, a child or young person detained in pursuance of—

(a) an order made by a court, or

(b) an order of recall made by the Secretary of State.

(2) Subsection (1) does not apply to—

(a) section 28;

(b) section 31;

(c) section 77;

(d) section 80;

(e) section 83;

(f) any amendment made by this Part of a provision which applies to, or in relation to, a child or young person detained in pursuance of—

(i) an order made by a court, or

(ii) an order of recall made by the Secretary of State.

(3) Regulations may apply any provision of this Part, with or without modifications, to or in relation to a child or young person detained in pursuance of—

(a) an order made by a court, or

(b) an order of recall made by the Secretary of State.

(4) The Secretary of State must consult the Welsh Ministers before making regulations under subsection (3) which will apply any provision of this Part to, or in relation to, a child or young person who is detained in Wales.

(5) For the purposes of this Part—

- "appropriate person", in relation to a detained person, means—

    (a) where the detained person is a child, the detained person's parent, or

    (b) where the detained person is a young person, the detained person;

- "detained person" means a child or young person who is—

    (a) 18 or under,

    (b) subject to a detention order (within the meaning of section 562(1A)(a) of EA 1996), and

    (c) detained in relevant youth accommodation, and in provisions applying on a person's release, includes a person who, immediately before release, was a detained person;

- "detained person's EHC needs assessment" means an assessment of what the education, health care and social care needs of a detained person will be on his or her release from detention;

- "relevant youth accommodation" has the same meaning as in section 562(1A)(b) of EA 1996, save that it does not include relevant youth accommodation which is not in England.

(6) For the purposes of this Part—

(a) "beginning of the detention" has the same meaning as in Chapter 5A of Part 10 of EA 1996 (persons detained in youth accommodation), and

(b) "the home authority" has the same meaning as in that Chapter, subject to regulations under subsection (7) (and regulations under section 562J(4) of EA 1996 made by the Secretary of State may also make provision in relation to the definition of "the home authority" for the purposes of this Part).

(7) For the purposes of this Part, regulations may provide for paragraph (a) of the definition of "the home authority" in section 562J(1) of EA 1996 (the home authority of a looked after child) to apply with modifications in relation to such provisions of this Part as may be specified in the regulations. 71Assessment of post-detention education, health and care needs of detained persons

(1) This section applies in relation to a detained person for whom—

(a) the home authority is a local authority in England, and (b) no

EHC plan is being kept by a local authority.

(2) A request to the home authority to secure a detained person's EHC needs assessment for the detained person may be made by—

(a) the appropriate person, or

(b) the person in charge of the relevant youth accommodation where the detained person is detained.

(3) Where this subsection applies, the home authority must determine whether it may be necessary for special educational provision to be made for the detained person in accordance with an EHC plan on release from detention.

(4) Subsection (3) applies where— (a) a request is

made under subsection (2), (b) the detained

person has been brought to the home

authority's attention by any person as someone

who has or may have special educational needs,

or

(c) the detained person has otherwise come to the home authority's attention as someone who has or may have special educational needs.

(5) In making a determination under subsection (3), the home authority must consult—

(a) the appropriate person, and

(b)the person in charge of the relevant youth accommodation where the detained person is detained.

(6)Where the home authority determines that it will not be necessary for special educational provision to be made for the detained person in accordance with an EHC plan on release from detention, it must notify the appropriate person and the person in charge of the relevant youth accommodation where the detained person is detained—

(a)of the reasons for that determination, and

(b)that accordingly it has decided not to secure a detained person's EHC needs assessment for the detained person.

(7)Subsection (8) applies where—

(a)the detained person has not been assessed under this section or section 36 during the previous six months, and

(b)the home authority determines that it may be necessary for special educational provision to be made for the detained person in accordance with an EHC plan on release from detention.

(8)The home authority must notify the appropriate person and the person in charge of the relevant youth accommodation where the detained person is detained—

(a)that it is considering securing a detained person's EHC needs assessment for the detained person, and

(b)that the appropriate person and the person in charge of the relevant youth accommodation where the detained person is detained each have the right to—

(i)express views to the authority (orally or in writing), and (ii)submit evidence to the authority.

(9)The home authority must secure a detained person's EHC needs assessment if, after having regard to any views expressed and evidence submitted under subsection (8), the authority is of the opinion that—

(a)the detained person has or may have special educational needs, and

(b)it may be necessary for special educational provision to be made for the detained person in accordance with an EHC plan on release from detention.

(10) After a detained person's EHC needs assessment has been carried out, the local authority must notify the appropriate person and the person in charge of the relevant youth accommodation where the detained person is detained of—

(a) the outcome of the assessment,

(b) whether it proposes to secure that an EHC plan is prepared for the detained person, and

(c) the reasons for that decision.

(11) Regulations may make provision about detained persons' EHC needs assessments, in particular—

(a) about requests under subsection (2);

(b) imposing time limits in relation to consultation under subsection (5);

(c) about giving notice;

(d) about expressing views and submitting evidence under subsection (8);

(e) about how detained persons' EHC needs assessments are to be conducted;
(f) about advice to be obtained in connection with a detained person's EHC needs assessment;

(g) about combining a detained person's EHC needs assessment with other assessments;

(h) about the use for the purposes of a detained person's EHC needs assessment of information obtained as a result of other assessments;

(i) about the use of information obtained as a result of a detained person's EHC needs assessment, including the use of that information for the purposes of other assessments;

(j) about the provision of information, advice and support in connection with a detained person's EHC needs assessment.

72 Securing EHC plans for certain detained persons

(1) Where, in the light of a detained person's EHC needs assessment it is necessary for special education provision to be made for the detained person in accordance with an EHC plan on release from detention, the home authority must secure that an EHC plan is prepared for him or her.

(2) Sections 37(2) to (5) and 38 to 40 apply in relation to an EHC plan secured under subsection (1) as they apply to an EHC plan secured under section 37(1), with the following modifications—

(a) references to "the child or young person" are to be read as references to the detained person,

(b) references to the local authority are to be read as references to the home authority, and

(c) references to the child's parent or the young person are to be read as references to the appropriate person.

(3) Section 33(2) to (7) apply where a home authority is securing the preparation of an EHC plan under this section as they apply where a local authority is securing a plan under section 37, with the following modifications—

(a) references to "the child or young person" are to be read as references to the detained person,

(b) references to the local authority are to be read as references to the home authority,

(c) references to the child's parent or the young person are to be read as references to the appropriate person, and

(d) the reference in subsection (2) to section 39(5) and 40(2) is to be read as a reference to those provisions as applied by subsection (2) of this section.

73 EHC plans for certain detained persons: appeals and mediation

(1) An appropriate person in relation to a detained person may appeal to the First-tier Tribunal against the matters set out in subsection (2), subject to section 55 (as applied by this section).

(2) The matters are—

(a) a decision of the home authority not to secure a detained person's EHC needs assessment for the detained person;

(b) a decision of the home authority, following a detained person's EHC needs assessment, that it is not necessary for special educational provision to be made for the detained person in accordance with an EHC plan on release from detention;

(c) where an EHC plan is secured for the detained person—

(i)the school or other institution named in the plan, or the type of school or other institution named in the plan;

(ii)if no school or other institution is named in the plan, that fact.

(3)The appropriate person may appeal to the First-tier Tribunal under subsection (2)(c) only when an EHC plan is first finalised for the detained person in accordance with section 72.

(4)Regulations may make provision about appeals to the First-tier Tribunal in respect of detained persons' EHC needs assessments and EHC plans secured under section 72, in particular about— (a)making and determining appeals;

(b)the powers of the First-tier Tribunal on determining an appeal; (c)unopposed appeals.

(5) A person commits an offence if without reasonable excuse that person fails to comply with any requirement—

(a)in respect of the discovery or inspection of documents, or (b)to

attend to give evidence and produce documents,

where that requirement is imposed by Tribunal Procedure Rules in relation to an appeal under this section.

(6) A person guilty of an offence under subsection (5) is liable on summary conviction to a fine not exceeding level 3 on the standard scale.

(7)Section 55(2) to (5) apply where an appropriate person intends to appeal to the First-tier Tribunal under this section as they apply where a child's parent or young person intends to appeal under section 51, with the following modifications—

(a)references to the child's parent or young person are to be read as references to the appropriate person, and

(b)references to mediation under section 53 or 54 are to be read as references to mediation with the home authority.

(8)Where, by virtue of subsection (7), the appropriate person has informed the mediation adviser that he or she wishes to pursue mediation with the home authority—

(a)the adviser must notify the authority, and

(b)the authority must—

(i)arrange for mediation between it and the appropriate person,

(ii)ensure that the mediation is conducted by an independent person, and

(iii)participate in the mediation.

For this purpose a person is not independent if he or she is employed by a local authority in England.

(9)Regulations under section 56 may make provision for the purposes of subsections (7) and (8) of this section, and accordingly section 56 has effect for those purposes with the following modifications—

(a)the references in subsection (1) to commissioning bodies are to be ignored;

(b)the reference in subsection (1)(e) to a child's parent is to be read as a reference to the parent of a detained person who is a child;

(c)the reference in subsection (1)(f) to the child's parent or young person is to be read as a reference to the appropriate person;

(d)in subsection (3), paragraphs (b) and (c) are to be ignored; (e)subsection (4)

is to be ignored.

74 Duty to keep EHC plans for detained persons

(1)This section applies in relation to a detained person—

(a)for whom a local authority in England was maintaining an EHC plan immediately before the beginning of his or her detention, or

(b)for whom the home authority has secured the preparation of an EHC plan under section 72.

(2)The home authority must keep the EHC plan while the person is detained in relevant youth accommodation.

(3)Regulations may make provision about the keeping of EHC plans under subsection (2), and the disclosure of such plans.

(4)The home authority must arrange appropriate special educational provision for the detained person while he or she is detained in relevant youth accommodation.

(5) If the EHC plan specifies health care provision, the detained person's health services commissioner must arrange appropriate health care provision for the detained person while he or she is detained in relevant youth accommodation.

(6) For the purposes of subsection (4), appropriate special educational provision is—

(a) the special educational provision specified in the EHC plan, or

(b) if it appears to the home authority that it is not practicable for that special educational provision to be provided, educational provision corresponding as closely as possible to that special educational provision, or

(c) if it appears to the home authority that the special educational provision specified in the plan is no longer appropriate for the person, such special educational provision as reasonably appears to the home authority to be appropriate.

(7) For the purposes of subsection (5), appropriate health care provision is— (a) the health care provision specified in the EHC plan, or

(b) if it appears to the detained person's health services commissioner that it is not practicable for that health care provision to be provided, health care provision corresponding as closely as possible to that health care provision, or

(c) if it appears to the detained person's health services commissioner that the health care provision specified in the plan is no longer appropriate for the person, such health care provision as reasonably appears to the detained person's health services commissioner to be appropriate.

(8) In this section, "detained person's health services commissioner", in relation to a detained person, means the body that is under a duty under the National Health Service Act 2006 to arrange for the provision of services or facilities in respect of the detained person during his or her detention.

75 Supply of goods and services: detained persons
(1) A local authority in England may supply goods and services to any authority or other person making special educational provision for a detained person, but only for the purpose set out in subsection (2).

(2) The purpose is that of assisting the local authority in the performance of a duty under section 74.

(3) The goods and services may be supplied on the terms and conditions that the authority thinks fit, including terms as to payment.

Information to improve well-being of children and young people with SEN

76 Provision and publication of special needs information

(1) The Secretary of State must exercise the powers listed in subsection (2) with a view to securing, in particular, the provision of special needs information which the Secretary of State thinks would be likely to assist the Secretary of State or others in improving the well-being of—

(a) children in England with special educational needs, and

(b) young people aged under 19 in England with special educational needs.

(2) The powers are those of the Secretary of State under the following provisions of EA 1996 (so far as relating to England)—

(a) section 29 (information from local authorities for purposes of Secretary of State's functions);

(b) section 408 (information in relation to maintained schools);

(c) section 537 (information about schools);

(d) section 537A (information about individual pupils);

(e) section 537B (information about children receiving funded education outside school);

(f) section 538 (information from governing bodies for purposes of Secretary of State's education functions).

(3) In each calendar year, the Secretary of State must publish, or arrange to be published, special needs information which has been obtained under EA 1996, where the Secretary of State thinks the publication of the information would be likely to assist the Secretary of State or others in improving the well-being of —

(a) children in England with special educational needs, and

(b) young people aged under 19 in England with special educational needs.

(4) Information published under subsection (3) must be published in the form and manner that the Secretary of State thinks fit, except that the names of the children and young people to whom the information relates must not be included.

(5) The Secretary of State may make a charge, or arrange for a charge to be made, for documents supplied by virtue of this section.

(6) A charge under subsection (5) must not exceed the cost of supply.

(7) "Special needs information" means—

(a) information about children, and young people, in England with special educational needs, and

(b) information about special educational provision made for those children and young people.

(8) References in this section to the well-being of children and young people with special educational needs are to their well-being so far as relating to—

(a) physical and mental health and emotional well-being;

(b) protection from abuse and neglect;

(c) control by them over their day-to-day lives;

(d) participation in education, training or recreation;

(e) social and economic well-being;

(f) domestic, family and personal relationships; (g) the

contribution made by them to society.

Code of practice

77 Code of practice

(1) The Secretary of State must issue a code of practice giving guidance about the exercise of their functions under this Part to—

(a) local authorities in England;

(b) the governing bodies of schools;

(c) the governing bodies of institutions within the further education sector;

(d) the proprietors of Academies;

(e) the management committees of pupil referral units;

(f) the proprietors of institutions approved by the Secretary of State under section 41 (independent special schools and special post-16 institutions: approval);

(g) providers of relevant early years education;

(h) youth offending teams;

(i) persons in charge of relevant youth accommodation;

(j) the National Health Service Commissioning Board;

(k)clinical commissioning groups;

(l)NHS trusts;

(m)NHS foundation trusts; (n)Local Health Boards.

(2)The Secretary of State may revise the code from time to time.

(3)The Secretary of State must publish the current version of the code.

(4)The persons listed in subsection (1) must have regard to the code in exercising their functions under this Part.

(5)Those who exercise functions for the purpose of the exercise by those persons of functions under this Part must also have regard to the code.

(6)The First-tier Tribunal must have regard to any provision of the code that appears to it to be relevant to a question arising on an appeal under this Part. 78Making and approval of code
(1)Where the Secretary of State proposes to issue or revise a code under section 77, the Secretary of State must prepare a draft of the code (or revised code).

(2)The Secretary of State must consult such persons as the Secretary of State thinks fit about the draft and must consider any representations made by them.

(3)If the Secretary of State decides to proceed with the draft (in its original form or with modifications), the Secretary of State must lay a copy of the draft before each House of Parliament.

(4)The Secretary of State may not take any further steps in relation to—

(a)   a proposed code unless the draft is approved by a resolution of each House, or

(b)   a proposed revised code if, within the 40-day period, either House resolves not to approve the draft.

(5)Subsection (6) applies if—

(a)both Houses resolve to approve the draft, as mentioned in subsection (4)(a), or
(b)neither House resolves not to approve the draft, as mentioned in subsection (4)(b).

(6)The Secretary of State must issue the code or revised code in the form of the draft, and it comes into force on such date as the Secretary of State may by order appoint.

(7) Subsection (4) does not prevent a new draft of a proposed code (or proposed revised code) from being laid before Parliament.

(8) In this section "40-day period", in relation to the draft of a proposed revised code, means—

(a) if the draft is laid before one House on a later day than the day on which it is laid before the other, the period of 40 days beginning with the later of the two days, and

(b) in any other case, the period of 40 days beginning with the day on which the draft is laid before each House.

(9) For the purposes of subsection (8), no account is to be taken of any period during which Parliament is dissolved or prorogued or during which both Houses are adjourned for more than four days.

79 Review of resolution of disagreements

(1) The Secretary of State and the Lord Chancellor must carry out a review of how effectively disagreements about the exercise of functions under this Part are being resolved.

(2) The Secretary of State and the Lord Chancellor must prepare a report on the outcome of the review.

(3) The Secretary of State and the Lord Chancellor must lay the report before Parliament before the end of the period of three years beginning with the earliest date on which any provision of this Part comes into force.

Supplementary

80 Parents and young people lacking capacity

(1) Regulations may apply any statutory provision with modifications, for the purpose of giving effect to this Part in a case where the parent of a child, or a young person, lacks capacity at the relevant time.

(2) Regulations under subsection (1) may in particular include provision for—

(a) references to a child's parent to be read as references to, or as including references to, a representative of the parent;

(b) references to a young person to be read as references to, or as including references to, a representative of the young person, the young person's parent, or a representative of the young person's parent;

(c) modifications to have effect in spite of section 27(1)(g) of the Mental Capacity Act 2005 (Act does not permit decisions on discharging parental responsibilities in matters not relating to a child's property to be made on a person's behalf).

(3) "Statutory provision" means a provision made by or under this or any other Act, whenever passed or made.

(4) "The relevant time" means the time at which, under the statutory provision in question, something is required or permitted to be done by or in relation to the parent or young person.

(5) The reference in subsection (1) to lacking capacity is to lacking capacity within the meaning of the Mental Capacity Act 2005.

(6) "Representative", in relation to a parent or young person, means —

(a) a deputy appointed by the Court of Protection under section 16(2)(b) of the Mental

Capacity Act 2005 to make decisions on the parent's or young person's behalf in relation to matters within this Part;

(b) the donee of a lasting power of attorney (within the meaning of section 9 of that Act) appointed by the parent or young person to make decisions on his or her behalf in relation to matters within this Part;

(c) an attorney in whom an enduring power of attorney (within the meaning of Schedule 4 to that Act) created by the parent or young person is vested, where the power of attorney is registered in accordance with paragraphs 4 and 13 of that Schedule or an application for registration of the power of attorney has been made.

81 Disapplication of Chapter 1 of Part 4 of EA 1996 in relation to children in England

Chapter 1 of Part 4 of EA 1996 (children with special educational needs) ceases to apply in relation to children in the area of a local authority in England.

82 Consequential amendments

Schedule 3 (amendments consequential on this Part) has effect.

83 Interpretation of Part 3

(1) In this Part—

- "EA 1996" means the Education Act 1996;

- "ESA 2008" means the Education and Skills Act 2008;

- "SSFA 1998" means the School Standards and Framework Act 1998.

(2) In this Part—

- "appropriate person" has the meaning given by section 70(5);
- "beginning of the detention" has the meaning given by section 70(6);
- "detained person" has the meaning given by section 70(5);
- "detained person's EHC needs assessment" has the meaning given by section 70(5);
- "education, health and care provision" has the meaning given by section 26(2);
- "EHC needs assessment" has the meaning given by section 36(2);
- "EHC plan" means a plan within section 37(2);
- "health care provision" has the meaning given by section 21(3);
- "the home authority" has the meaning given by section 70(6) (subject to subsection (7) of that section);
- "mainstream post-16 institution" means a post-16 institution that is not a special post-16 institution;
- "mainstream school" means—

(a) a maintained school that is not a special school, or

(b) an Academy school that is not a special school;

- "maintained school" means—

(a) a community, foundation or voluntary school, or

(b) a community or foundation special school not established in a hospital;

- "post-16 institution" means an institution which—

(a) provides education or training for those over compulsory school age, but

(b) is not a school or other institution which is within the higher education sector or which provides only higher education;

- "proprietor", in relation to an institution that is not a school, means the person or body of persons responsible for the management of the institution;

- "relevant early years education" has the meaning given by section 123 of SSFA 1998;

- "relevant youth accommodation" has the meaning given by section 70(5);
- "social care provision" has the meaning given by section 21(4);
- "social services functions" in relation to a local authority has the same meaning as in the Local Authority Social Services Act 1970;

- "special educational needs" has the meaning given by section 20(1);

- "special educational provision" has the meaning given by section 21(1) and (2);

- "special post-16 institution" means a post-16 institution that is specially organised to make special educational provision for students with special educational needs;

- "training" has the same meaning as in section 15ZA of EA 1996;
- "young person" means a person over compulsory school age but under 25.

(3) A child or young person has a disability for the purposes of this Part if he or she has a disability for the purposes of the Equality Act 2010.

(4) A reference in this Part to "education"—

(a)includes a reference to full-time and part-time education, but

(b) does not include a reference to higher education, and "educational" and "educate" (and other related terms) are to be read accordingly.

(5) A reference in this Part to—

(a) a community, foundation or voluntary school, or (b) a community or foundation special school, is to such a school within the meaning of SSFA 1998.

(6) A reference in this Part to a child or young person who is "in the area" of a local authority in England does not include a child or young person who is wholly or mainly resident in the area of a local authority in Wales.

(7) EA 1996 and the preceding provisions of this Part (except so far as they amend other Acts) are to be read as if those provisions were contained in EA 1996.

Printed in Great Britain
by Amazon